SIGNS in Judaism

A Resource Book for the Jewish Deaf Community

Adele Kronick Shuart

Illustrated by Ruth E. Peterson

Edited by Muriel Strassler

Published for

National Congress of Jewish Deaf

by

BLOCH PUBLISHING CO. INC., NEW YORK

Because this book contains God's word and prayers, please treat it with respect.

Copyright ® 1986 by Adele Kronick Shuart
and National Congress of Jewish Deaf

All rights reserved. No part of this book may be reproduced without written permission from the publisher.

Published for National Congress of Jewish Deaf by Bloch Publishing Company, Inc.

Manufactured in the United States of America

Library of Congress Cataloging-in-Publication Data

Shuart, Adele Kronick
    Signs in Judaism

    Bibliography: p.
    Includes Index.

    1. Sign language––Dictionaries. 2. Judaism––Customs and practices––Terminology. 3. Judaism––Customs and practices. 4. English language––Dictionaries––Hebrew. 5. English language––Dictionaries––Yiddish. I. National Congress of Jewish Deaf (U.S.) II. Title.
HV2475.S529 1986   419'.02403924   86-17155
ISBN 0-8197-0505-05 (pbk.)

Dedicated to the Jewish Deaf Community

SIGNS IN JUDAISM

Table of Contents

Acknowledgements VII

Foreword IX

Introduction XI

History of Jewish Religion for the Deaf XIII

Affiliates of the National Congress of Jewish Deaf XVII

CATEGORIES XIX

    Biblical and Historical Jewish Personalities 1

    Biblical and Jewish Places and History 19

    General Ritual Objects 33

    Holidays 39

    Jewish Life 69

    Languages 92

    Life Cycles 94

    Modern Israel 105

    Prayers 112

        Vocabulary 112

        General Blessings/Prayers 128

        Songs 131

    Sabbath 133

    Sanctuary 138

    Traditional Jewish Food 148

    Yiddish Expressions 156

APPENDICES 158

    Ten Commandments 159

    Eighteen Benedictions 159

    Fingerspelling used in Israel 160

    Hebrew Alphabet and Gematria 161

    Hebrew Months 162

    Holidays According to Jewish Year 162

    Pentateuch 163

    Psalm 23 163

    Twelve Tribes 164

References 165

Index 167

Acknowledgements

This book was made possible in part by a grant from the Laurent Clerc Cultural Fund Book of the Gallaudet College Alumni Association. Generous contributions were also received from the Endowment Fund of the National Congress of Jewish Deaf; Hebrew Union Seminary, Cincinnati, Ohio; Mr. and Mrs. Morris Fink; Lillian Hanover and Gertrude Yawitt.

This book would not be possible without the excellent input from Resource Committee members: Rabbi Moshe Ebsetin; Rabbi Douglas Goldhamer; Rabbi Elyse Goldstein; Rabbi Alan Henkin; Rabbi Mark Hurvitz; Rabbi Jeffrey Perry-Marx; Dr. Susan Fisher, Linguist; Dr. Nancy Frishberg, Linguist; Simon J. Carmel, Anthropologist; Carl Chopinsky, Interpreter; Joyce Groode, Interpreter; Sharon Neuman Solow, Interpreter; Rose Zucker, Interpreter and Jewish Educator; Marcia Goldberg, Jewish Educator; Toby Marx, Jewish Educator; Laura Nadoolman, Jewish Educator; Meyer Lief, Deaf Jewish Religious Teacher; Betty Oshman, Deaf Jewish Leader; Marla Petal, Community Service Consultant; Celia Warshawsky, Deaf Jewish Leader; Yetta Abarbanell, Deaf Jewish Leader and Dr. Martin Sternberg, author of **American Sign Language Dictionary**.

Much credit is due to four leaders of the National Congress of Jewish Deaf who have provided guidance during the years of this book's development: Gerald Burstein, Alvin Klugman, Kenneth Rothschild and Alexander Fleischman.

Others who have given generously of their time and services are: The Board of Jewish Education of Greater Washington, Rabbi Mark Levine; Rabbi Joseph Katz and Sara Simon; Rabbi Matthew Simon; Ellie Gellman; Karen and Miriam Speedone; Hava Savir and Israel Sela; Aldon Fruge; Ira Lerner; George Schroeder; Rabbi Steven Bayar; Rabbi Daniel Grossman; Dr. William Stokoe; Dr. Lester Waldman; Dr. Trenton Batson; Barry Strassler and Nancy Torbett.

During the periods of sign collection, we were very appreciative to those who offered office space and homes for photo sessions: Marcella Meyer and Marge Klugman for use at Greater Los Angeles Council on Deafness, Inc.; the homes of the Cecil Weinstocks in Queens, NY; the Bruce Herzigs, Lori Kronick and the Herbert Rosens in Maryland.

A vote of thanks also goes to the models whose likeness are illustrated in the book and to the photographers whose work made the illustrations possible. The models were Nettie Kishineff and David Perlovsky of California; Alfred and Margaret Solomon and Cecil and Sylvia Weinstock of New York; Elaine and Bruce Herzig, Lori Kronick and Steve and Susy Rosen of Maryland. The photographers were David Balacier, Carl Bravin, Simon J. Carmel, Elaine and Bruce Herzig and Lynn Jacobowitz.

Acknowledgements

This book was made possible in part by a grant from the Laurent Clerc Cultural Fund Book of the Gallaudet College Alumni Association. Generous contributions were also received from the Endowment Fund of the National Congress of Jewish Deaf; Hebrew Union Seminary, Cincinnati, Ohio; Mr. and Mrs. Morris Fink; Lillian Hanover and Gertrude Yawitt.

This book would not be possible without the excellent input from Resource Committee members: Rabbi Moshe Ebstein; Rabbi Douglas Goldhamer; Rabbi Elyse Goldstein; Rabbi Alan Henkin; Rabbi Mark Hurvitz; Rabbi Jeffrey Perry-Marx; Dr. Susan Fisher, Linguist; Dr. Nancy Frishberg, Linguist; Simon J. Carmel, Anthropologist; Carl Chopinsky, Interpreter; Joyce Groode, Interpreter; Sharon Neuman Solow, Interpreter; Rose Zucker, Interpreter and Jewish Educator; Marcia Goldberg, Jewish Educator; Toby Marx, Jewish Educator; Laura Nadoolman, Jewish Educator; Meyer Lief, Deaf Jewish Religious Teacher; Betty Oshman, Deaf Jewish Leader; Celia Warshawsky, Deaf Jewish Leader; Yetta Abarbanell, Deaf Jewish Leader and Dr. Martin Sternberg, author of **American Sign Language Dictionary**.

Others who have given generously of their time and services are: The Board of Jewish Education of Greater Washington, Rabbi Mark Levine; Rabbi Joseph Katz and Sara Simon; Rabbi Matthew Simon; Ellie Gellman; Karen and Miriam Speedone; Hava Savir and Israel Sela; Aldon Fruge; Ira Lerner; George Schroeder; Rabbi Steven Bayar; Rabbi Daniel Grossman; Dr. William Stokoe; Dr. Lester Waldman; Dr. Trenton Batson; Barry Strassler and Nancy Torbett.

During the periods of sign collection, we were very appreciative to those who offered office space and homes for photo sessions: Marcella Meyer and Marge Klugman for use at Greater Los Angeles Council on Deafness, Inc.; the homes of the Cecil Weinstocks in Queens, NY; the Bruce Herzigs, Lori Kronick and the Herbert Rosens in Maryland.

A vote of thanks also goes to the models whose likeness are illustrated in the book and to the photographers whose work made the illustrations possible. The models were Nettie Kishineff and David Perlovsky of California; Alfred and Margaret Solomon and Cecil and Sylvia Weinstock of New York; Elaine and Bruce Herzig, Lori Kronic and Steve and Suzy Rosen of Maryland. The photographers were David Balacier, Carl Bravin, Simon J. Carmel, Elaine and Bruce Herzig, and Lynn Jacobowitz.

Foreword

With the growth and development of the National Congress of Jewish Deaf and its affiliates, there has been a parallel growth of interest in, and observance of, Jewish religious customs in the Jewish Deaf community. This has, in turn, created a demand by rabbis, religious educators, interpreters and other interested persons, for a comprehensive book on Jewish religious signs.

Adele Kronick Shuart has painstakingly researched the significance and meaning of Jewish holiday and Sabbath customs and observances in an effort to give authenticity to the book. As a linguist and a teacher of sign language, she has been sensitive to the feelings of the Jewish Deaf Community regarding existing signs. She has consulted and employed experts in the fields of sign language, religion and art and has used their contribution creatively and constructively.

The publication of **Signs in Judaism** is a high watermark for the National Congress of Jewish Deaf. It answers the quest for a presentation of the structure and content of Jewish religious signs. It illustrates the rich history and heritage of the deaf Jew. It is a valuable addition to the lexicon of signs and will serve as an important resource to those of all faiths living and working in the deaf community.

MARGE KLUGMAN
Editor, **The Congregation News**
Temple Beth Solomon of the Deaf

Los Angeles, California
May, 1986

Introduction

The National Congress of Jewish Deaf (NCJD) has recognized the need for a published work which includes signs for Judaic purposes. In 1978, the Congress set a mandate for a book to be developed to enhance the religious education and services for Jewish deaf and hearing-impaired children and adults, hereafter called the Jewish Deaf Community. The factors that led to this development were the lack of a published book on Judaic signs, the lack of information or training in the concepts of Judaism, the lack of signs based on Judaic concepts, and little exposure to Jewish education among the Jewish Deaf Community.

"Without knowledge, there is no understanding, without understanding, there is no knowledge."

"Im ed da'at, en binah, im en binah, en da'at."

Pirkei Avot 3:21

The areas of concern included keeping the Judaic tradition, that interpretation based on Torah and Talmud be made clear, and that Hebrew or Yiddish be translated or transliterated into American Sign Language (ASL).

Signs in Judaism: A Resource Book for the Jewish Deaf Community does not intend to replace other good sign language books on the market. Instead, it is to serve as a supplement to interested users in the Jewish Deaf Community. As an educational tool, it is not designed as a dictionary of signs, nor is it designed for a beginning signer, but rather as a resource book from which the members of the Jewish Deaf Community can benefit.

It is hoped that this much-needed book generates interest among student rabbis in working with Jewish deaf individuals, and that rabbis, teachers and family of deaf and hearing-impaired children, and interpreters, will use it to improve religious services. That it will help individuals working with deaf and hearing-impaired children to promote their spiritual growth. And last, but not least, that this book will help any interested person — hearing, deaf, or hearing-impaired — gain some knowledge of the religious, historical, and cultural background of Judaism.

Introduction

As mentioned, there has been no work published in Judaic concepts expressed in American Sign Language, which has been found to be the true language of the American deaf community. What is American Sign Language? Ms. Ann Silver (1985) has given a concise definition of ASL which states:

> "The signs in ASL are word-like units which have both concrete and abstract meanings. Signs are made by either one or both hands assuming distinctive shapes in particular locations and executing specified movements. The use of spatial relations, directions, orientations, and movement of the hands, as well as facial expression and body shift, make up the grammar of ASL."

During the process of researching this book, many people asked for Israeli signs, requesting that the author check with Israel for their signs. However, American Sign Language is older than Israeli Sign Language and many signs have already been developed and become traditional signs. Similarly, there have been inquiries regarding "Jewish Sign Language". There is no Jewish Sign Language as there is no "English Sign Language". There is British Sign Language, American Sign Language, and Israeli Sign Language, among others. The signs in this book can be considered religious signs or American Judaic signs. There are borrowed signs, though, especially those that are name signs in Israel.

This book includes background information, text, Hebrew or Yiddish transliterations, English, Hebrew or Yiddish words, illustrated signs, sign gloss, signs of regional variations, borrowed signs from Israel, and cross references for similar signs for some words.

To maintain the spelling of Hebrew and Yiddish transliterations has been difficult. To keep the transliteration in Sephardic Hebrew forms compounds the problem. The experts on the West Coast often disagree with the experts on the East Coast. This difference parallels the regional variations in sign language.

Regional variations means that a sign for a certain concept may differ in various regions of the United States. It is not the intent of the author to standardize or universalize the signs, just as no one would try to standardize the pronunciation of some words uttered in New England, or in the South. The attempt at standardization killed Latin.

In American Sign Language, signs do change. In this book, the variations are noted. There are some signs which are contrary to the Judaic concept expressed, yet are considered traditional signs. This book is non-judgemental unless a sign does not follow American Sign Language or Judaic principles. The signs shown in this book are preferred Judaic-related signs. Linguistically speaking, the acceptance of signs belongs to the Jewish Deaf Community.

It will be noted by the reader that not every word in the book has a sign, nor is every sign illustrated. It is beyond the scope of this book to include all existing signs. As mentioned, some words that have similar signs as other words are cross-referenced. There are words that have sign gloss which do not have illustrations.

History of Jewish Religion for the Deaf

As stated in **The Jewish Deaf** "Historical Notes..." that in Holland, Germany (1843), England (1750's) and Austria (1844), religious education was provided for Jewish deaf children. The first three nations gave instruction in Hebrew, while in Austria, the concepts of Judaism, Jewish ideas, and man's duty to God and the Ten Commandments were taught. Dr. Deutsch of Austria (1867) believed that there were no difference in the learning capacities of Jewish deaf children and those of Jewish hearing children. The method of teaching, though, has always been a problematic issue.

Late 1910's — Early 1930's in the United States

New York City was the leader in providing and maintaining religious education and services for Jewish deaf pupils and adults. The pupils from the New York Institution for the Instruction of the Deaf (Fanwood Institution), as reported in the **Jewish Deaf**, attended religious classes and services at the Communal Center for the Jewish Deaf, Temple Beth Israel and Temple Emanuel.

Interestingly, much report was made on the confirmation services that were conducted in sign language at the Fanwood Commencement services. Few reports were published regarding Bar Mitzvah. No mention was made in regard to teaching Hebrew to these pupils.

Since the number of pupils was so large during that period, there was no way that they could be given individual religious education, though it was ideal. As David Kaplan, in his column, "Organization of Religious Classes for Children" in **The Jewish Deaf** (Vol. II, 1916) stated, they came to a "happy medium" by organizing the classes into three groups based on age, language capabilities and grade in school.

The leaders in the efforts to ensure that Jewish deaf pupils received a religious education were Rabbi Amateau and Rev. DeSola Pool. There were several noted instructors who were deaf during this period: Louis A. Cohen, Samuel Kohn and Max Lubin. Meyer Lief later assumed a leadership role.

Each year the graduating class from Fanwood had Confirmation services at the Communal Center on West 115th Street, New York City. In June 1917, an article appeared in the **Harlem Home News,** when 54 pupils in their school military uniforms, marched from the Institution on West 163rd Street and Fort Washington Avenue to West 115th Street to attend Confirmation and Commencement Exercises.

The number of pupils attending the religious education program at Fanwood was at one time 100. The number of Jewish deaf people attending Friday night services ranged from 400 to 600 (622 in June 1916).

History of Jewish Religion for the Deaf

In 1918-1920, there was concern about the lack of a prayer book for the Jewish deaf. A group from the Council of Jewish Women (CJW) led by Mrs. Rose Goldsmith Stern who spent almost two years simplifying the prayer book so that the deaf "with their very limited vocabulary" could benefit. It sold for 35 cents per booklet. In the February 1920 edition of the **Jewish Deaf**, Mrs. Stern, in her column, expressed her concern that the New York Jewish deaf group never purchased the number of copies expected. She was surprised because, in her opinion, it was in the "simplest English for the use of the deaf". This booklet, however, had no illustration of signs.

1940's — 1950's

New York City was still the center of deaf Jewish life in America through the 1940's and 1950's. The New York Hebrew Association of the Deaf conducted regular Sabbath services under the auspices of New York Society for the Deaf funded by Federation of Jewish Philanthropies.

In late 1950's the Jewish leaders of the deaf from all over the United States realized there was a need to join together a common bond—— to foster Judaism among the Jewish deaf and establish a national organization. They were Philip Hanover, Leonard Warshawsky, Alexander Fleischman, Bernard Teitelbaum and Mrs. Anna Plapinger. The formation of National Congress of Jewish Deaf (NCJD) in 1956 would not be made possible without the personal financial backing by Mrs. Anna Plapinger to fund the convention. She is fondly called the "Mother of NCJD".

This organization meets biennially at conventions and several accomplishments to date are:

- ——**NCJD QUARTERLY,** a newsletter published quarterly,
- ——Endowment Fund to provide financial assistance to any interested rabbinical candidate with the sign language training,
- ——the creation of the office of Executive Director,
- ——the creation of a Certificate of Merit to an outstanding member of each affiliate given at the convention,
- ——the creation of the Plapinger Endowment Fund to an outstanding deaf Jewish leader,
- ——the NCJD Archives,
- ——the NCJD Hall of Fame, which honors deaf Jewish leaders or personalities for their accomplishments/contributions to the Jewish deaf community.

History of Jewish Religion for the Deaf

1960's — 1980's

By the 1960's Jewish deaf leaders were seeking self-determination in conducting their own services and as a result several congregations of the deaf were formed, beginning with Temple Beth Solomon of the Deaf in California in 1960; Temple Beth Or of the Deaf in New York in 1961; and the formation of Congregation Bene Shalom as an adjunct of the Chicago Hebrew Association of the Deaf in 1972.

The formation and stability of these congregations, run by deaf people themselves, played a large part in the rebirth of interest in religious services by other NCJD affiliates and by deaf Jewish individuals living away from the larger population centers.

Although Jewish rabbinical seminaries and schools do not, as yet, include sign language or studies on deafness as part of their curriculum, many students and ordained rabbis have worked with the deaf and the number of persons in the Jewish religious community familiar with the needs of the hearing impaired is constantly growing. There were and are some deaf rabbis. One who was trained at the Hebrew Union Seminary in Cincinnati, Ohio, unfortunately did not live to become an ordained rabbi for NCJD. His name was Alton Silver. The three known hearing impaired and deaf rabbis in the 1980's are Rabbi David Rabinowitz of Michigan, Rabbi Fred Friedman of Baltimore, MD. of the Orthodox branch, and Daniel Grossman of Staten Island, NY of the Reconstructionist branch.

Moreover, the common bond of fostering the Judaism among the Jewish Deaf Community expanded internationally when the World Organization of Jewish Deaf was formed in 1977.

By the 1980's interpreted services become more common as more congregations made their facilities accessible to hearing impaired and deaf persons as well as persons with other disabilities.

Lastly, one of the primary goals of the National Congress of Jewish Deaf is to educate and disseminate information to the hearing sector and to bring, once again, to the Jewish deaf nationwide, the Jewish education and pride in heritage that was once so readily available to deaf Jewish New Yorkers in the early 1900's.

Contributed by:
Alexander Fleischman
Marge Klugman
Adele Kronick Shuart

NATIONAL CONGRESS OF JEWISH DEAF

Affiliates:

Hebrew Association of the Deaf of New York
Congregation Bene Shalom of Hebrew Association of the Deaf
　　　of Chicago
Hebrew Association of the Deaf of Cleveland
Hebrew Association of the Deaf of Los Angeles
Hebrew Association of the Deaf of Philadelphia
Boston Hebrew Association of the Deaf
Brooklyn Hebrew Society of the Deaf
Jewish Deaf Society of Baltimore
Temple Beth Or of the Deaf
Jewish Students Association of Gallaudet College
Temple Beth Solomon of the Deaf
Washington Society of Jewish Deaf
Beth Torah of the Deaf
Jewish Community Center Association of the Deaf
Hearing Impaired Chavura at Rochester
Toronto Jewish Society for Hearing Impaired

Associate Affiliates:

New York Society for the Deaf
Chabad House Hearing Impaired Program
Judaica Captioned Film Center, Inc.

CATEGORIES

Key to abbreviations:

s. – singular
pl. – plural

m. – masculine
f. – feminine

Y – Yiddish

BIBLICAL AND HISTORICAL JEWISH PERSONALITIES

This chapter deals with personalities from the Biblical and Jewish historical period alphabetically ranging from Adam and Eve to Twelve Tribes.

As mentioned in the introduction, not every word has a sign nor an illustration of a sign. However, there are some non-illustrated words such as "Angels" and "Prophets" which may be found in other sign language resource books.

The illustrated name signs in this chapter were gathered during the author's sign collection trips from the leading Jewish deaf communities such as the New York City, Los Angeles and Washington, DC areas. As a result, there are variations in name signs.

As discussed at the 1982 NCJD Convention Workshop in Washington, DC, the names should be spelled first, then followed by name signs. In different regions, a name sign can be developed which may be acceptable within the concept of American Sign Language along the line of Judaic concept. What are illustrated in this chapter are the sample name signs that are preferred by the Jewish Deaf Community in different regions. As said at the Workshop mentioned above, it has been a desire that there be one universal name sign for each personality in the Biblical and Historical period. It would not be an easy task to universalize a name sign. As students of linguistics in sign language, we know that the community accepts only the signs that they feel comfortable with. If NCJD were to conduct a survey on which name signs are acceptable universally, it would take forever.

Aaron   Aharon   אַהֲרֹן

An older brother of Moses; the first High Priest (Kohen) who officiated in the Tabernacle, especially in the Holy of Holies.
See also: Holy of Holies; Tabernacle.

Adam and Eve   Adam and Havah   אָדָם וְחַוָה

First man created on Earth and first woman created from Adam's rib who ate forbidden fruit (tree of knowledge of good and evil) and who were banished from the Garden of Eden.
See also: Garden of Eden.

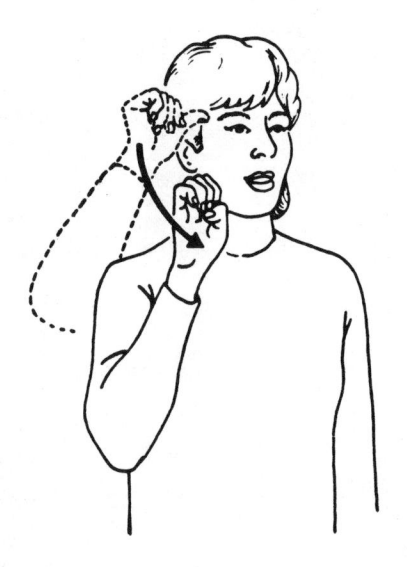

Adam and Eve
"A" handshape at side of a temple moves down into "E" handshape at side of chin.
Author's note: Use this sign when mentioning these two people simultaneously. These signs are almost unusable when used individually.

Angel(s)   Malakh(im)   מַלְאָכִים

Messenger(s) of God (not in human form) who delivers God´s word to people.

Sign for Angel is found in other excellent sign language resource books.

Bath-Sheba   Bat-Sheva   בַּת־שֶׁבַע

Wife of King David; mother of Solomon.

Cain, Abel and Seth   Kayin, Hevel and Shet   קַיִן, הֶבֶל וְשֵׁת

Children of Adam and Eve. Cain, the first man born on Earth, was the farmer who killed brother Abel, a shepherd. Seth was born after Abel´s murder.

"Mark of Cain" - a symbol for greed and sin.

Children of Israel   Benai Yisra´el   בְּנֵי יִשְׂרָאֵל

An historic name for Jewish people; also means Israelite nation.

See also: Israel; Jacob.

David   David Ha-Melekh   דָּוִד הַמֶּלֶךְ

A young boy who killed Goliath; was secretly anointed as King by Samuel; wrote many Psalms; conquered Jerusalem. It is said that the Messiah will be a descendant from the House of David.

See also: Goliath.

David
"D" handshape at the opposite shoulder moves down diagonally to waist.

Deborah   Devorah   דְּבוֹרָה

A judge and prophetess who led Israelites in war against the Canaanites. A full story is described in the Book of Judges. "Song of Deborah" is one of the oldest poems in Hebrew literature.

Elijah   Eliyahu   אֵלִיָּהוּ

The zealous prophet, 9th century B.C.E., who was opposed to idolatry; was most popular, most dramatic and most romantic among the Jewish prophets.

See also: Idol/Idolatry; Elijah's Cup (Passover); Elijah's Chair (Circumcision).

Elijah
"E" handshape in "prophet" sign, then closed "5" handshape at sides of body move straight down.
Clue: "Prophet" + "Person".

Esau   Esav   עֵשָׂו

Twin brother of Jacob and son of Isaac; the hunter.

See also: Jacob; Patriarchs.

Ezra   עֶזְרָא

A priest and scribe who restored the Torah to Israel after the return from the Babylonian Exile; arranged Torah reading on Mondays and Thursdays; a member of the Great Assembly (Sages).

Goliath   Golyat   גָּלְיָת

A Philistine giant who was killed by David with a slingshot and a stone.

See also: David.

Hebrew(s)   Ivri(m)   עִבְרִי(ם)

Abraham was the first Hebrew; the name given to Jewish people in ancient Jewish history; then changed to Israelites and now Jews.

See also: Jews; Hebrew (Languages).

See JEW for sign for Hebrew(s).

High Priest   Kohen Gadol   כֹּהֵן גָּדוֹל

The leading hereditary office of Temple Service. Aaron was the first High Priest.

See also: Aaron; Holy of Holies, Kohen.

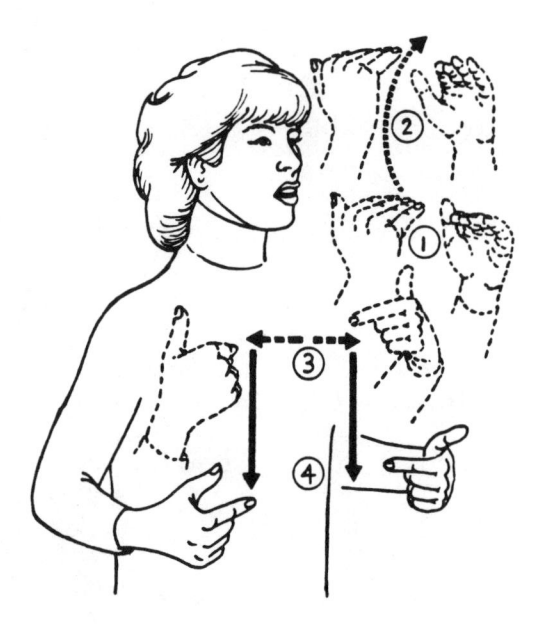

High Priest
1. + 2. "High", then
3. "L" handshapes point at each other at the center of chest at the chest level, then move away in opposite direction, then downward.

Other Variation
"High" + "Rabbi".
Clue: Priest wearing a breastplate.

Ishmael   Yishmaʹel   יִשְׁמָעֵאל

A stepbrother of Isaac; firstborn son of Abraham and Hagar,
who was Sarah's handmaiden. Ishmael's descendants were the
Arabs.

Israel   Yisraʹel   יִשְׂרָאֵל

Name given to Jacob; descendants of sons of Jacob were called
Israelites.

See also: Jacob; Children of Israel; Hebrews.

See Illustration, Variation 3, in "Biblical and Jewish Places and
   History".

Israel Variation 1
"I" handshape touching downward once on either side of the chin.
This sign may be related to people (Israelis or Israelites).

Israel Variation 2
"I" handshape in circular movement in space.
The person agent may be added to represent the citizens of Israel.

See Variation 3 in "Biblical and Historical Jewish Personalities".

7

Israelites   Benai Yisra´el   בְּנֵי יִשְׂרָאֵל

See: Hebrews; Levites; Children of Israel; Israel; Jews.

See above for sign.

Jew(s); Jewish   Yehudi(m)   (ם)יְהוּדִי

Developed from the name for the members of the tribe of Judah. After the Roman exile, the Israelites became known as Jews.

See also: Israelites; Judea; Hebrews.

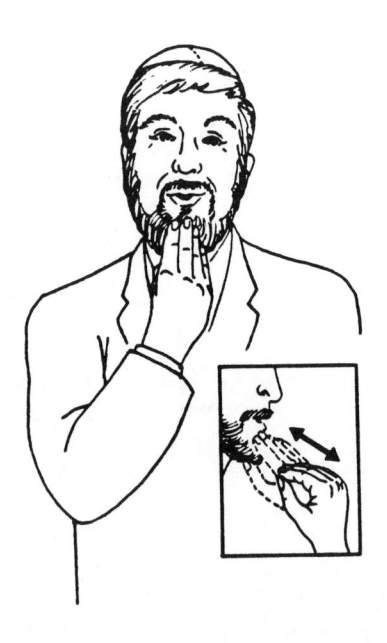

Jew(ish), Hebrew, Israel
Bent "B" handshape at the chin moves down closing four fingers and thumb.
Other Variation:
"People" + "Torah".

Jew(ish), Hebrew, Israel
(Israel version)
Closed, slightly bent "5" handshape brushes down on the chin twice.

Joseph   Yosef   יוֹסֵף

Eleventh son of Jacob; the first son of Rachel; sold into Egyptian slavery by jealous brothers; interpreted dreams for the Pharaoh; reunited with his family in Egypt when they escaped famine.

Kohen (Kohanim)   Priest(s)   כֹּהֵן (כֹּהֲנִים)

During the early period of the Jewish history until the fall of the Second Temple, Kohanim were important in Jewish life. At that time, their duties were to offer sacrifices. Their

responsibilities declined after the Temple was destroyed. Today some of the duties are reminiscent of their past history.
See also: Aaron; Holy of Holies; Levites; Israelites; High
         Priests; Kohen in "Sanctuary".

Levi   Levi   לֵוִי

Third son of Jacob and Leah; an ancestor of the Levite Tribe.
See also: Levites.

Levites   Levi´im   לְוִיִּים

Descendants of Levi, served under Kohanim in the Holy Temple.
See also: Israelites; Kohanim; Levi.

Lot   לוֹט

Nephew of Abraham and who accompanied him to Canaan; lived in Sodom with his wife and only he, his wife and two daughters were saved from fire of destruction but his wife, who looked back at Sodom despite the warnings, became a pillar of salt. See also: Sodom and Gomorrah.

Matriarchs   Arba Imahot (Four Mothers)   אַרְבַּע אִמָּהוֹת

    Sarah   Sarah   שָׂרָה

Formerly Sarai; wife of Abraham; mother of Isaac.

    Rebecca   Rivkah   רִבְקָה

Wife of Isaac; mother of Esau and Jacob.

    Rachel   Rahel; Rochel   רָחֵל

First wife of Jacob; mother of Joseph and Benjamin (Binyamin).

    Leah   Le´ah   לֵאָה

Sister of Rachel; second wife of Jacob; mother of six Tribes (Reuven, Shimon, Levi, Yehuda, Yissachar, and Zevulun).

Messiah   Mashiah   מָשִׁיחַ

In Hebrew, it means "anointed"; in Biblical times the High Priest and King were anointed; later the term referred to a redeemer who would bring salvation to Jewish people and the entire world. The Prophet Elijah will announce the Messiah.
See also: Elijah.

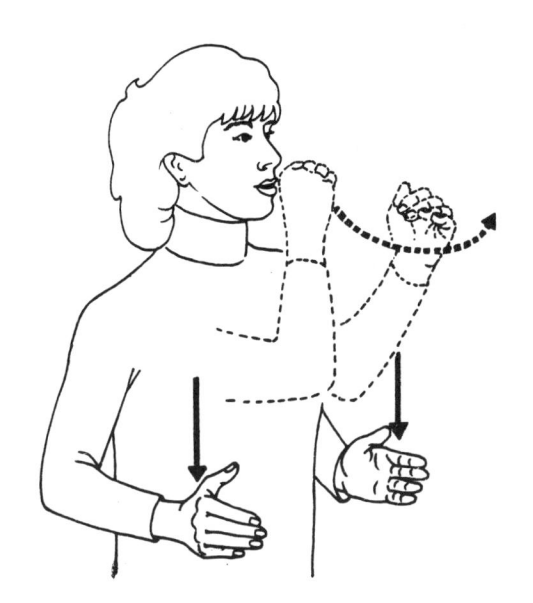

Messiah
Sign "Prophet" with "M" handshape, and then closed "5" handshapes at sides of body move straight down.
Western version
"M" in King movement.
Eastern version
"M" in Savior movement.

Miriam   Miryam   מִרְיָם

Sister of Moses and Aaron and who put baby Moses in the Nile River to save him from Pharaoh's order to kill the firstborn male babies; led Israelite women in singing and dancing after crossing the divided Red Sea. Because of her good deeds, God gave the Israelites a well of water for their use in their wanderings in the wilderness.
See also: Moses; Red Sea.

Moses   Moshe   מֹשֶׁה

The man who led the Jewish people from Egypt, led them to Mount Sinai where he received the Ten Commandments, and led people for 40 years in the wilderness. Subject of one of the most dramatic and inspiring stories in the Bible.

See also: Ten Commandments; Mount Sinai; Egypt; Red Sea.

Moses   Eastern Version
"M" handshape taps against the opposite palm, then moves down and taps again on the palm.
Clue: "Commandment" concept.
Other variations:
"M" in Wisdom movement.
"M" handshape circled as in Insurance movement.

Naomi   נָעֳמִי

An Israelite mother-in-law of Ruth, the Moabite; the story is told in Book of Ruth.

See also: Ruth.

Patriarchs	Avot (Fathers)	אָבוֹת
Abraham	Avraham Avinu	אַבְרָהָם אָבִינוּ

The father of Jewish people, originally called Abram (Avram); the first man to recognize and preach the belief in One God. God requested the sacrifice of his son Isaac to test his faith, but he was spared. He founded the morning prayer (Shaharit).

See also: Hebrews; Isaac.

Abraham Variation 1
The right "A" handshape in the would-be stabbing movement is caught by the left hand by the wrist.
Western Version
"A" handshape circles in space as in Insurance sign.

Abraham Variation 2
 (Israel Version)
With left arm in horizontal position in front of body, right "A" moves in circular movement in front of the left arm.
Clue: Shield over left arm.

Isaac   Yitzhak   יִצְחָק

The only son of Abraham and Sarah and whom Abraham offered for sacrifice as a test of Abraham's faith in God, but was spared; husband of Rebecca; he founded the afternoon prayer (Minhah).

See also: Abraham.

Isaac
Little finger stabs at the side of the neck.
This sign was developed at 1982 NCJD Convention Workshop.

Jacob   Ya´akov   יַעֲקֹב

   also called Israel   Yisra´el

A son of Isaac and Rebecca, husband of Rachel and Leah; father of 12 sons; dreamed he saw a ladder going up to heaven; tricked his father, Isaac, into giving a special blessing to him instead of to the firstborn, Esau. He founded the evening prayer (Ma´ariv).

See also: Israel; Isaac; Esau.

Note: All of the names of the Patriarchs are mentioned in prayers.

Sign: With each handshape in small circular movement in space as follows: "A", "I" + "J".

Pharaoh   Par´oh   פַּרְעֹה

During the Biblical days, this was the name or the title for the rulers in Egypt. "Pero" means "Great House".

See also: Exodus; Egypt.

Pharaoh
Bent closed "5" handshapes at top of the head move down and touch the shoulders.
Other Variations:
-With the same movement as above, use "P" handshapes.
-"Egypt" + "King".

Pharisees   Perushim   פְּרוּשִׁים

During the period of the Second Temple, a political/religious party which was flexible in the interpretation of the Jewish law with regards to the needs of the times, claimed the Torah was for everyone - not just the Priests or the rich; established free, required, Jewish education for all children.

Priest(s)   Kohen (Kohanim)   כֹּהֵן (כֹּהֲנִים)

From the early period of Jewish history they were responsible for offering sacrifices in the Temple. Kohanim still have special rights and restrictions.

See also: High Priest; Israelites: Levites: Aaron; Kohen in
          "Biblical & Historical Personalities" and "Sanctuary".
See HIGH PRIEST for root sign for "Priest".

Prophets   Nevi´im   נְבִיאִים

From the period of Moses to the early days of the Second Temple, there were two roles the prophets performed every generation. They functioned as the ones who brought the word of God to the people of Israel, and were able to project the future based on actions of the people.

See also: Elijah; Moses.

Ruth   Root   רוּת

A Moabite woman who was a famous convert to Judaism and who followed Naomi, her Israelite mother-in-law, home to Bethlehem when Ruth's husband died; an ancestress of David. This story which is told in Book of Ruth, is usually read on Shavuot.

See also: Naomi; Shavuot.

Sadducees   Tzedukim   צְדוּקִים

The political/religious party which was composed of those who believed only in the literal interpretation of the Torah.
See also: Pharisees.

Samson   Shimshon (Shimshon Ha-Gibbor)   שִׁמְשׁוֹן הַגִּבּוֹר

A Nazirite (one who was forbidden to cut his hair or drink alcoholic beverages); last of Judges in Israel; represents strength.

Samuel   Shemuel   שְׁמוּאֵל

The prophet who led the people before the Kings; chose and anointed Saul and David as King.

Saul   Shaul   שָׁאוּל

First King of Israel.

Solomon   Shelomo Ha-Melekh   שְׁלֹמֹה הַמֶּלֶךְ

Son of David and Bath-sheba; third King of Israel known for his wisdom; wrote Book of Proverbs, Kohelet (Ecclesiastes) and Song of Songs; built the Holy Temple.

See next page for illustration.

King Solomon
"K" handshape at the opposite shoulder moves down diagonally into "S" handshape to waist.
Other Variation:
With the same movement as above, use the "S" handshape.

Twelve Tribes   Shevatim   שְׁנֵים עָשָׂר שְׁבָטִים

Sons of Jacob, whose descendants were organized into the clans of the Israelite nation. Each tribe received a portion of the land of Canaan except Levi. The full list and map are found in the Appendix.

BIBLICAL AND JEWISH PLACES & HISTORY

This chapter includes the words and illustrated signs related to Biblical and Jewish places and history in alphabetical order from the Ark of the Covenant to Mount Zion.

Some illustrated signs as indicated in the sign gloss in this chapter are borrowed from Israel. They are: Beersheba, Bethlehem, Hebron, Jerusalem and Syria.

Ark of the Covenant   Aron Ha-Berit   אֲרוֹן הַבְּרִית

A chest which held the Ten Commandments; carried by the Levites during the Israelites' wanderings; rested in the Tabernacle during this period. After conquering Canaan, it was placed in the sanctuary in Shiloh; then brought to Jerusalem by David and then placed in the Holy of Holies of the Holy Temple by King Solomon.

See also: Holy Temple; Tabernacle; Holy of Holies; Solomon.

Babylonia   Bavel   בָּבֶל

Located in Middle East; was an important center of Jewish life and culture for about 1,000 years, after the destruction of the Temple.

Beersheba   Be´er Sheva   בְּאֵר־שֶׁבַע

An ancient city where Abraham and Isaac made treaties and Jacob brought offerings to God.

Beersheba   Israel Version
Closed "5" handshapes in space at face level with palms facing each other; move down in V shape movement touching the bottom of both hands above the waist level.

Beth El   House of God   בֵּית־אֵל

A place of worship; a town between Jerusalem and Shechem where Abraham and Jacob built altars.

Bethlehem   Bet Lehem   בֵּית־לֶחֶם

Sacred to both Jews and Christians; near where Rachel is buried; the birthplace of David.

See next page for illustration.

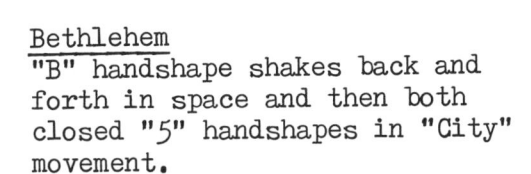

Bethlehem
"B" handshape shakes back and forth in space and then both closed "5" handshapes in "City" movement.

Bethlehem   Israel Version
"City" + "Bread".

Canaan   Kena´an   כְּנַעַן

An early name for Palestine; later Israel; the land between Jordan and the Mediterranean; also called the Holy Land and the Promised Land.

See also: Israel; Palestine; Judah/Judea.

Cities of the Plain   Arey Ha-Kikkar   עָרֵי הַכִּכָּר

Sodom, Gomorrah, Admah, Zeboiim and Zoar, the wicked cities which were destroyed by fire except for Zoar which was saved for Lot's sake. Now at the bottom of the Dead Sea.

See also: Sodom and Gomorrah; Lot.

Dead Sea (Sea of the Plain)   Yam Ha-Melah (the Salty Sea)

יַם הַמֶּלַח

A sea 1,292 feet below sea level; ruins of the Cities of the Plain are at the bottom. The Dead Sea Scrolls were found near it.

See also: Cities of the Plain; Sodom and Gomorrah.

Egypt   Mitzrayim   מִצְרַיִם

A land rich in Jewish history beginning with Abraham; during the Exodus under Moses, the Jewish people were freed from slavery in Egypt. The Jews had relations with Egypt during the period of the First Temple.

See also: Abraham; Exodus; Moses.

Egypt
"X" handshape taps at the top of the forehead twice.
Other Variation:
"E" handshapes at sides of forehead move outward and down touching each other below the chin.

Exodus   Yetziat Mitzrayim   יְצִיאַת מִצְרַיִם

Freedom of the Jews from the Egyptian bondage; narrated in the Book of Exodus

See also: Egypt; Moses.

Exodus   Variation 1
1. "Escape" sign
2. Wiggle fingers moving out.

Exodus   Variation 2
1. "Save" movement.
2. Open "5" handshapes wiggle out.

Galilee   Galil   גָּלִיל

Northern part of present day Israel. In the Talmud, it was divided into the valley, Upper Galilee and Lower Galilee. People of Galilee were considered "people of the land" (am ha-aretz); very patriotic fighters against the tyranny of Rome.

Galut   Exile   גָּלוּת

Compulsory (forced) exile of the Jews from Israel after the destruction of the First and Second Temples. Also means "Diaspora". Traditionally, it means all who live outside of the Land of Israel. Modern Hebrew uses "Tefutsot" instead of "Galut". Alternate Hebrew form Golah.

See also: Diaspora; Tefutsot.

Garden of Eden   Gan Ayden   גַּן־עֵדֶן

A paradise where Adam and Eve resided and from which they were expelled after disobeying God's order not to eat any "fruit" from the Tree of Knowledge; Hebrew phrase means the ideal life after death.

See also: Adam and Eve.

Hebron   Hevron   חֶבְרוֹן

One of the four sacred (holy) cities; where the tombs of the
Patriarchs and Sarah, Rebecca and Leah are located.
See also: Patriarchs; Holy Cities of the Halukah; Matriarchs.

Hebron   Israel Version
Soft "5" handshapes at the
sides of jaw move down twice
almost touching little
fingers.

Holy Cities of the Halukah   Arey Ha-Halukah עָרֵי הַחֲלוּקָה

Sacred cities of Jerusalem; Tiberias; Safed and Hebron.
Jerusalem was the first as the Temple of Solomon and later
the Second Temple were built there. The great supreme court
of the Jews (Sanhedrin) was established there. After the
destruction of the Second Temple, the Sanhedrin settled in
Tiberias. Safed was known for its pious schools for the
study of Kabbalah, and Hebron for its Grave of Makhpelah
where the Patriarchs and Matriarchs were buried.
See also: Hebron; Jerusalem; Matriarchs; Patriarchs.

Holy of Holies   Kodesh Ha-Kodashim   קֹדֶשׁ הַקֳּדָשִׁים

A most holy place in the Tabernacle, then in the Temple where the Ark of the Covenant was; entered only by the High Priest on Yom Kippur.

See also: Ark of the Covenant; High Priest.

Holy Land   Eretz Ha-Kodesh   אֶרֶץ הַקֹּדֶשׁ

See: Canaan; Israel; Palestine.

Holy Temple   Bet Ha-Mikdash   בֵּית הַמִקְדָשׁ

Refers to the First and Second Temple in Jerusalem. The First Temple had the Ark of the Covenant brought into it by King Solomon and was destroyed on the 9th of Av, 586 B.C.E. by Babylonians. The Second Temple, which was destroyed in 70 C.E. by the Romans, had two sections which were: the outer or Holy Place, and the inner or Holy of Holies. Before the destruction of the Temple, the Jews visited it at least three times a year (Passover; Shavuot and Sukkot).

See also: Holy of Holies; Solomon; Tisha B´Av.

Sign: "Holy" + "Temple".

Idol/Idolatry   Avodah Zarah   עֲבוֹדָה זָרָה

Idol worship was widespread prior to Moses´ receiving the Ten Commandments. In later years, Elijah was opposed to this renewed

practice among the Israelites. During the Greek and Roman periods, idolatry was widely practiced among the Hellenists and the Romans.
See also: Elijah.

Israel   Eretz Yisra´el   אֶרֶץ יִשְׂרָאֵל

Land given by God to Abraham; land of Biblical Israel. During the time of the Jewish Monarchy the northern Kingdom was called Israel, the southern Kingdom was called Judah.
See also: Palestine; Canaan; Judah.

Israel Variation 3
"I" handshape moves in half arc, then taps on the back of the opposite hand. (Establishment of the State of Israel); Zion.
See Variations 1 and 2 in "Biblical and Historical Jewish Personalities".

Jericho   Yeriho   יְרִיחוֹ

A fortified city in ancient history near Jerusalem where, as told in the Book of Joshua, the walls of Jericho crumbled from the sound of the Israelites´ trumpets.

Jerusalem   Yerushalayim   יְרוּשָׁלַיִם

A city which was conquered by David from the Jebusities; David's capital; and where the Ark was brought to rest. David wanted to build the First Temple there. The site of the First and Second Temples; one of the holy cities.

See also: Holy Cities; Ark of the Covenant; David; the Holy Temple.

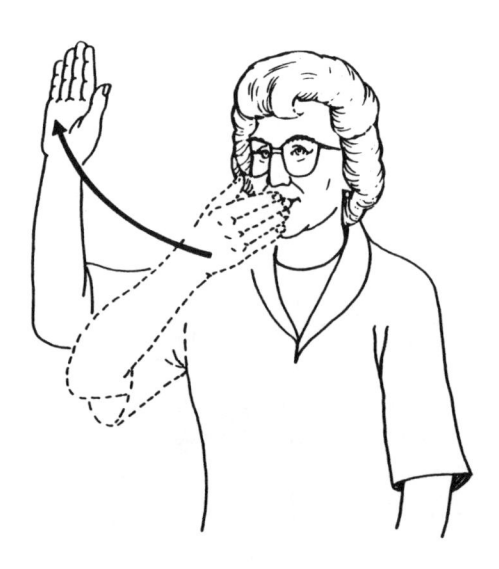

Jerusalem   Israel Version
Closed "5" handshape kisses lips and moves out; then touches space as though touching the Western Wall.
Other variations:
- Kissing lips and moving out may be repeated.
- Sign: "J" + "City".

Jordan   Yarden   יַרְדֵן

A river in Palestine - a natural dividing line between the east and west through the Sea of Galilee to the Dead Sea.

Judah/Judea   Yehudah   יְהוּדָה

Son of Jacob whose descendants became one of the 12 tribes. Later the name of the Kingdom ruled by King David's sons. The Romans named the country Judea during the period of the Second Temple.

See also: Jew(s).

Land of Israel   Eretz Yisra´el   אֶרֶץ יִשְׂרָאֵל

See: Israel.

Masada   Metzadah   מְצָדָה

A fortress where 900 Jewish patriots made their last stand in the war against Rome. Symbol of Jewish resistance to tyranny.

Masada
"M" handshapes touch each other in front at chest level, then right "M" moves wavingly down to the right side.

Mount Sinai   Har Sinai   הַר סִינַי

The mountain where Moses received the Ten Commandments.

See also: Moses; Ten Commandments.

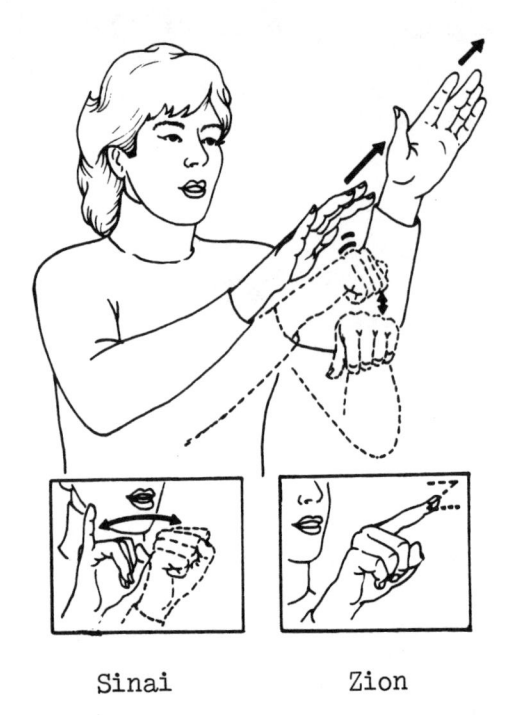

Mount Sinai and Mount Zion
Root sign for Mount...
"A" handshape taps at top of the opposite fist, then open into soft "5" handshapes moving upward and out.
Then Sinai using "S" into "I" handshape drawing in the air.

For Zion use index finger drawing "Z" in the air.
"Sinai" and "Zion" may be fingerspelled.

Sinai   Zion

Palestine   אֶרֶץ יִשְׂרָאֵל

A land first named Canaan in the Bible; also called Palestine or the Land of Israel. After 1917, British controlled Palestine until 1948. Originally on both sides of Jordan River, then the British called the east bank TransJordan.

See also: Canaan; Jordan; Israel; Holy Temple.

Persia   Paras   פָּרַס

The story of Queen Esther took place in this great empire. Modern name is Iran.

See also: Purim; Queen Esther.

Red Sea (Sea of Reeds)   Yam Soof   יַם סוּף

The scene where a miracle took place when the Israelites crossed the sea on dry land under the guidance of Moses in their escape from Egypt.

See also: Exodus; Egypt; Moses.

Sodom and Gomorrah   Sedom Va-Amorah   סְדֹם וַעֲמוֹרָה

Two of the Cities of the Plain where people led wicked lives. God decided to destroy them through fire and brimstone. Lot, who lived in Sodom, was warned to leave with his family.

See also: Cities of the Plain; Lot.

Syria   Suria   סוּרְיָה

An ancient nation where the King Antiochus and his men fought against the Maccabees in 165 B.C.E.

LEFT
Syria   Israel Version 1
Tips of index, middle and ring fingers tap against the opposite palm twice.

RIGHT
Syria   Israel Version 2
Index fingers pointing up at chin moves down twice.

Tabernacle   Mishkan or Ohel Mo´ed   מִשְׁכָּן, אֹהֶל מוֹעֵד

During the Israelites´ wandering in the wilderness, they carried what was called a tent or portable sanctuary (tabernacle). It took less than six months to build it. Later on, the First Temple was built by King Solomon in Jerusalem to replace the Tabernacle.

See also: Ark of the Covenant; Holy of Holies; the Holy Temple; Solomon.

Western Wall (Wailing Wall)   Kotel Ma´aravi   כֹּתֶל הַמַעֲרָבִי

The only remaining section of the Holy Temple in Jerusalem where many Jews come to pray; the modern Jews call it the "Western Wall". The archeologists believe it is a part of the Second Temple.

See also: Holy Temple; Tisha B´Av.

See sign gloss for Western Wall under Jerusalem.

Mount Zion   Har Tzeyon   הַר צִיוֹן

A hill in Jerusalem where David´s tomb is located; later it became a symbol for Jerusalem and Israel.

See also: David.

See sign gloss for Mount Zion under Mount Sinai.

GENERAL RITUAL OBJECTS

This chapter includes objects traditionally used in everyday Jewish life. The items used in Sanctuary are listed in the <u>Sanctuary</u> chapter.

The illustration of a person wearing the yarmulka, tallit and tefillin is included. One may develop a mime/iconic sign for each item.

<u>Hanukat Ha-Bayit</u>   <u>Dedicating a New Home</u>   חֲנוּכַּת הַבַּיִת

Upon moving in a new home, a mezzuzah is attached to the doorpost and a special blessing (shehecheyanu) is said. Certain items are given to symbolize:

1) hope that there will always be enough to eat - Bread
2) light and joy - Candles
3) reminder of Temple sacrifices - Salt
4) joy and sweetness - Honey

<u>See also</u>: Mezzuzah; Shehecheyanu.

<u>Kiddush Cup</u>   <u>Cup of Benediction</u>   Kos Shel B´rakhah

כּוֹס שֶׁל בְּרָכָה

Wine cup/goblet used for saying Kiddush. See Kiddush in "Sabbath" for explanation.

<u>Kippah</u>   <u>Skullcap</u>   כִּפָּה

See Yarmulka [Y] for illustration and explanation.

Mahzor   מַחֲזוֹר

Holiday prayer book based on Siddur and piyyutim (religious hymns)

See also: Siddur.

Mezzuzah   מְזוּזָה

A small case is attached on the right doorpost of a Jewish home or building. Inside the case is a parchment containing two paragraphs from the Torah (the Sh´ma). They tell us that we should love God and obey God´s Commandments.

See also: Hanukat Ha-Bayit.

Mezzuzah
"G" handshape moves straight down on the opposite palm.

Phylacteries

See Tefillin for illustration and explanation.

Prayer Book   Siddur   סִדּוּר

A year-round prayer book used by Orthodox, Conservative, Reform and Reconstructionists. Each group has its own version.

See also: Mahzor.

Prayer Shawl

See Tallit for illustration and explanation.

Pushke [Y]   Tzedakah Box   פּושקע

By tradition, it is in every Jewish home where family members put money in for some charitable purpose. A member usually puts money in before lighting the Sabbath candles. These boxes are also found in synagogues, cemeteries and other Jewish public places.

See also: Tzedakah.

Siddur   סִדּוּר

See Prayer Book.

Star of David   Magen David   מָגֵן דָּוִד

A six-pointed star symbolizing Judaism; an emblem of State of Israel; the Shield of David.

See next page for illustration.

Star of David
Double "D" handshapes move up in "Star" movement.
Other Variation:
"Jewish" + "Star".

Tallit   Prayer Shawl   טַלִית

Worn by men during the morning service every day of the year, and during the evening of Yom Kippur. In recent years some women have been wearing them, too.

Tallit Katan   Small Tallit   Arba Kanfot   טַלִית קָטָן

A small tallit worn by religious males under their shirts every day. Yiddish - Arba Kanfes.

Tefillin   Phylacteries   תְּפִילִין

Two small leather boxes - one worn on forehead (Shel Rosh) and the other on the left arm (Tefillin Shel Yad). Worn during the morning services on weekdays. Traditionally, the males use them after their 13th birthday. In each box are the verses from the Torah (the Sh´ma). The act of binding is important spiritually -- not physically. It connects mind, heart and body.

Tzitzit   Fringes   צִיצִית

The fringes on the Tallit and Tallit Katan hanging from the corners of the Tallit which are used to kiss the Torah when the Scrolls are carried around or when blessings are recited over the Torah. The four fringes symbolize the four corners of the earth. The knotted fringes symbolize the 613 mitzvot.
See also: Tallit; Tallit Katan.

Yarmulka   Kippah   כִּפָּה   יַרמלקע

A skullcap or head covering worn for reciting prayers or reading religious books and for religious rituals; worn constantly by observant Jews to remind them of God´s presence.

See next page for illustration.

1. <u>Yarmulka</u>
   Cupped "5" handshape pats on head twice.

2. <u>Tallit</u>
   Soft "C" handshapes at chest area move down to approximate waist line.

3. <u>Tefillin</u>
   One hand in soft "A" handshape in winding motion around the opposite forearm or hand twice. Also sign for "Bar/Bat Mitzvah".

HOLIDAYS

(for Holidays in order of the year, see Appendix)

Holidays start at sunset the night before (Erev).

This chapter covers the traditional holidays of the year broken into the three parts which are: High Holy Days, Pilgrim Festivals and Minor Festivals.

HIGH HOLY DAYS   YAMIM NORA´IM   יָמִים נוֹרָאִים

Rosh Hashanah   Jewish New Year   רֹאשׁ הַשָּׁנָה

It begins in the first day of the Jewish month of Tishri. Orthodox, Conservative and some Reform Jews observe for two days, while other Reform Jews observe it only one day. It celebrates the anniversary of creation. Jews pray to be written in the Book of Life for the new year. Also called Yom Ha-Zikaron (Day of Remembrance), Yom Teru´ah (Day of Blowing the Shofar) and Yom Ha-Din (Day of Judgement).

See also: Yom Kippur.

Custom: Hallah dipped in honey to mean that next year will be sweet.

Tashlih -- Orthodox Jews go to the nearest body of water and empty pockets, a symbol of casting off their sins.

Shanah Tovah -- Happy New Year.

Le-Shanah Tovah Tikatevu -- "May you be inscribed for a new
       year!"

May sign "New Year" or sign using "R" + "H" in similar movement as in "New Year".

Shofar   Ram's Horn   שׁוֹפָר

It summons people to prayer and repentance; used also at the Ne'ilah service on Yom Kippur. The person who blows the shofar is Ba'al Teki'ah. In the past, in Israel, it was used to sound every Friday afternoon to remind people the Sabbath was coming. Today, they use the loudspeakers before the Sabbath.

See also: Ne'ilah; Yom Kippur.

Shofar
Soft "S" handshapes at top of each other at lip; then the right hand moves out in arc into "C" handshape.

Akedah   Binding of Isaac   עֲקֵדָה

The Biblical story read during the service on Rosh Hashanah relates how God tested Abraham by commanding him to take his son Isaac to the top of Mount Moriah and offer him as a sacrifice.

See also: Abraham; Isaac.

Selihot   סְלִיחוֹת

A collection of prayers asking for forgiveness; also means the special, late night service held one week before Rosh Hashanah when the prayers for forgiveness are recited.

Ten Days of Penitence   Aseret Yemai Teshuvah   עֲשֶׂרֶת יְמֵי תְּשׁוּבָה

The days between Rosh Hashanah and Yom Kippur; time for repentance and spiritual return.

Yom Kippur   Day of Atonement   יוֹם כִּפּוּר

The holiest day of the Jewish year; the last day of Ten Days of Penitence; a most solemn day on which the Jews fast and pray for forgiveness including confession of their sins.

Custom: Orthodox Jews do not wear leather and wear a kitel
        (white robe).

See next page for illustration.

Yom Kippur
Fist taps on chest in the heart area twice.
Also sign for "Repent".
Western Variation
Using the same movement, use "Y" + "K".
See other variation of "Repent" in "Vocabulary".

Al Het   עַל חֵטְא

Confessional prayers chanted several times by the whole congregation.

Ashamnu   אָשַׁמְנוּ

"We have sinned." Twenty-four (24) sins recited in alphabetical order. Written in the plural to show group responsibility.

Avodah   עֲבוֹדָה

Part of Yom Kippur service which describes the history of the ritual in the Temple performed by the High Priest.

Fast   Tzom   צוֹם

Abstaining from eating as a form of repenting for sins. See "Fast" in "General Terms Used in Holidays" at the end of this chapter.

Kol Nidre (Aramaic)   All Vows   כָּל נִדְרֵי

The service which begins the eve of Yom Kippur; a prayer/statement asking God to void all vows made rashly during the next year.

Ne´ilah   Closing   נְעִילָה

The closing service of Yom Kippur, right before the "Gates of Heaven are closed and the Book of Life is sealed." (When God makes decisions and seals the fate of all people.)

PILGRIM FESTIVALS   SHALOSH REGALIM   שָׁלֹשׁ רְגָלִים

In the Biblical days, every male Israelite was required to go to Jerusalem three times a year during Passover, Shavuot and Sukkot to make sacrifices at the Holy Temple.

Passover   Festival of Unleavened Bread   Pesah   פֶּסַח

The eight-day celebration begins on the 15th day of Nissan to mark the Exodus of Israelites from Egyptian slavery led by Moses. Also called Hag Ha-Aviv (Spring Holiday), Zeman Herutenu (Time of Our Freedom).

See also: Exodus; Pharaoh; Moses; Red Sea.

See next page for illustration.

Seder   Order   סֵדֶר

The Passover ritual dinner during which the story of Exodus is told and special foods are eaten. The Seder is held on the first two nights in the United States and only first night in Israel.

Passover Variation 1
    (Traditional)
Matzah Variation 1
    (Traditional)
"A" handshape taps at the
opposite elbow.
Other variation:
"P" handshape at elbow
using the same movement as
above.
See Matzah Variation 2
in this chapter.

Passover Variation 2
1. "P" handshape over the
   wrist of the opposite
   hand, then
2. "S" handshape in "Save"
   movement.
This sign was developed in
1972 NCJD Workshop.

Passover Variation 3
Evolved from Passover
Variation 2. The "Save"
movement is dropped. "P"
handshape moves over the
wrist of the opposite
hand.

45

Seder Plate   Ke´arah   קְעָרָה

With permission from Ila Cherney, My Haggadah
Behrman House, Inc. 1986.

חֲרֹסֶת Haroset   מָרוֹר Maror

בֵּיצָה Baitzah

זְרוֹעַ Zero´ah   כַּרְפַּס Karpas

Hazeret -- lettuce -- a symbol of bitter herbs in
    addition to horseradish.
Salt water -- a reminder of the tears of the Jews
    during their sufferings as slaves.

Haggadah   Story of Passover   Haggadah Shel Pesah
Haggadot (pl.)
הַגָּדָה שֶׁל פֶּסַח

The book recited during the Seder telling the story of how the Jews escaped from Egyptian bondage to Israel under the leadership of Moses.

See also: Moses; Seder; Exodus; Egypt.

Haggadah
Double "H" handshapes almost touching each other move out in arc, palms facing up.
Other variation: "Passover" + "Book".

The Four Questions   Arba Kushiyot   Fir Kashes [Y]
אַרְבַּע קֻשְׁיוֹת   פִיר קַשִׁיוֹת

The Four Questions are asked by the youngest person in the room. In different ways they ask why Pesah is being celebrated. "Mah nish-tannah ha-lailah ha-zeh?": "Why is this night different from all other nights?"

See also: Haggadah.

Matzah   Matzot (pl.)   Unleavened Bread   מַצָּה (מַצּוֹת)

Thin, flat unleavened bread made from flour and water in remembrance of the escape from Egypt when the Jews did not have time to wait for the bread dough to rise. At the Seder, three pieces of matzah are placed along the Seder plate. They symbolize the three classes in the Jewish people: Cohen, Levi and Israel. More recently, additional pieces of matzah are used to remember the Holocaust and the Jews in the Soviet Union.

See also: Kohen; Levi; Israel.

See Passover Illustration, Variation 1, for

   Matzah Illustration, Variation 1.

Matzah   Variation 2
"M" handshape taps at the opposite elbow.
See Passover Variation 1 for Matzah Variation 1.

Maror
"M" handshape at a corner
of the mouth turns in half
arc and stop.
Clue: "Bitter" movement.
Other variations:
"Bitter" + "Green" or
"Bitter" + "Food".

Afikoman   Hidden Matzah   אֲפִיקוֹמָן

The middle matzah of the three matzot is taken out and broken in half. One half (afikoman) is hidden. A child who finds the missing piece is rewarded. This missing piece is broken and distributed among the guests at the Seder to be eaten at the end of the meal. The Seder cannot be concluded until the afikoman is returned and eaten.

Four Cups of Wine   Arba Kosot   אַרְבַּע כּוֹסוֹת

The four cups of wine drunk at the Seder are a reminder of the four acts of redemption which God performed:

"I shall bring you out."

"I will deliver you."

"I will free you."

"I will take you."

Elijah's Cup   Kos Shel Eliyahu   כּוֹס שֶׁל אֵלִיָּהוּ

An extra wine cup placed on the Seder table for Elijah, the Prophet. As the legend says, Elijah will come and announce the coming of the Messiah. Family opens the door to welcome him.

Ten Plagues   Eser Makkot   עֶשֶׂר מַכּוֹת

At the Seder, each person dips a finger or spoon in and out of a cup of wine when each plague is mentioned. Since wine is a symbol of joy, we take wine out from the cup to show we are sorry that God had to send ten plagues against the Egyptians.

Blood	Dam	דָּם
Frogs	Tzefar-day-a	צְפַרְדֵּעַ
Gnats	Kinim	כִּנִּים
Wild Beasts	Arov	עָרוֹב
Blight	Dever	דֶּבֶר
Boils	Sheheen	שְׁחִין
Hail	Barad	בָּרָד
Locusts	Arbe	אַרְבֶּה
Darkness	Hosheh	חֹשֶׁךְ
Slaying of the First Born	Makat Behorot	מַכַּת בְּכוֹרוֹת

Dayenu   "It would have been sufficient."   דַּיֵּנוּ

A song about God's many rewards to the Israelites.

Had Gadya   One Kid   חַד גַּדְיָא

A ballad in Aramaic at the end of the Seder which relates the chain of events which started when a father bought a kid (baby goat). Some say that the father is a symbol for God and the kid is a symbol for the Jewish people.

Next Year in Jerusalem   Leshanah Ha-Ba´ah Be-Yerushalayim

לְשָׁנָה הַבָּאָה בִּירוּשָׁלָיִם

Said at the conclusion of the Seder service in expression of hope for better times and that one day we will all be reunited in Jerusalem and Israel.

Next Year in Rebuilt Jerusalem   לְשָׁנָה הַבָּאָה בִּירוּשָׁלַיִם הַבְּנוּיָה

Leshanah Ha-Ba´ah Be-Yerushalayim Ha-Benuyah

This has also been added to some modern Haggadot since the reunification of Jerusalem.

Hametz   Leaven   חָמֵץ

Foods that are forbidden at Passover (e.g. foods made with yeast, dough allowed to rise, many foods from grain).

Custom: Bedikat   Hametz   Search for Leaven   בְּדִיקַת חָמֵץ

   An old tradition in which the night before Passover eve, the head of household uses a candle looking for hametz. He then uses a feather to sweep the leaven and burns the leaven the next morning saying a special prayer.

Shavu´ot   <u>Feast of Weeks</u>   שָׁבוּעוֹת

Festival which takes place seven weeks after Passover; celebration in remembrance of the Jewish people receiving the Ten Commandments on Mount Sinai. The Book of Ruth is read on this holiday. Furthermore, it celebrates the spring harvest and the planting of the summer crop. In ancient Israel the people brought their first fruits (Bikkurim) to the Temple on Shavu´ot. More recently, Confirmation is celebrated during this period.

<u>See also</u>: Lag B´Omer, Ten Commandments.

<u>Shavuot</u>
"7" handshape on opposite palm moves straight out as in "Week" movement.
<u>Other variation</u>:
"S" handshape in "Week" movement.

<u>Akdamut</u>   אַקְדָמוּת

An Aramaic poem recited during Shavuot before the reading of the Torah.

Sukkot   Festival of Booths   סֻכּוֹת

An eight-day festival which starts on the 15th day of Tishri in the Diaspora celebrating the harvest with the building of the sukkah and using the Four Species. This concludes the High Holiday season. In Israel, it is celebrated for seven days. See also: Four Species; Sukkah.

Sukkot
"A" handshapes touching each other shake back and forth. One-hand movement may be used.
Other Variation:
Two hands interlocked overhead move from back to front to symbolize the roof of the sukkot. Also a sign for "Lulav".

Sukkah   Booth   סֻכָּה

A booth, decorated with fruits and vegetables, is built to remind us that the Israelites lived in a booth-like shelter during their 40 years of wandering in the wilderness after the Exodus from Egypt, and before entering Israel. It is also a reminder that the ancient Israelite farmers built shelters in the field during the fall harvest rather than walk back and forth between the fields and their homes.

The Four Species   Arba´ah Minim   אַרְבָּעָה מִנִים

It is the custom during Sukkot to gather together the Four Species which symbolize that all Jews are bound together:

    Lulav (palm) -- backbone   לוּלָב

    Etrog (citron) -- heart   אֶתְרוֹג

    Hadass (myrtle) -- eyes   הֲדַס

    Aravah (willow) -- lips   עֲרָבָה

Some say that bringing together these four different species symbolizes that all people, whether they are wise or not, observant or not, are bound together in the eyes of God.

Lulav   לוּלָב

It is the custom on each morning of Sukkot except Shabbat to wave the lulav in all directions which symbolize that God is everywhere. Since all Four Species are to be used during Sukkot, the myrtle and willow are tied to the lulav so they can be waved too. The etrog is held in the hand, during the waving.

See Sukkot for sign gloss.

Hakkafot   Processionals   הַקָּפוֹת

While celebrating the end of the reading of the Torah, people dance and carry the Torah around the sanctuary seven times.

See also: Hoshanah Rabbah; Simhat Torah.

Hoshanah Rabbah   Seventh Day of Sukkot   הוֹשַׁעְנָא רַבָּא

This day ends three weeks of penitence which started on Rosh Hashanah. On this day, people parade around the sanctuary seven times singing Hoshanah (pleas for salvation).

See also: Hoshanot; Hakkafot; Simhat Torah.

Hoshanot   הוֹשַׁעְנוֹת

Series of poems from Psalms read during Sukkot and Hoshanah Rabbah while circling the synagogue carrying the Four Species.

See also: Hoshanah Rabbah; Four Species.

Simhat Torah   Rejoicing of the Torah   שִׂמְחַת תּוֹרָה

The last day of Sukkot when reading the Torah for the year is finished and started over again. The concept of this is that reading the Torah is never-ending. This marks the end of the High Holiday season. The Jews dance with the Torah as it is carried around seven times. It is a custom that everyone in the synagogue be called up to the Torah on this day.

Simhat Torah
1. Double "A" handshapes start at palms facing each other in space move in rolling movement to touching each other and then,
2. the dominant hand moves straight out while the other hand remains in stationary position.

Other Variation:
"Torah" + "Celebrate".

Hatan Torah   חָתָן תּוֹרָת

The person who has the honor of reading the end of the Torah.

Kallat Torah   כַּלַת תּוֹרָה

Women who are called upon to read the end of the Torah.

Hatan Berayshit   חָתָן בְּרֵאשִׁית

The person who reads the beginning of the Torah.

Kallat Berayshit   כַּלַת בְּרֵאשִׁית

Women who are called upon to read the beginning of the Torah.

See also: Hakkafot; Hoshanah Rabbah.

Kol Ha-Ne´arim   כָּל הַנְעָרִים

All the children are called up to the Torah. In some
synagogues, they stand under a large tallit.

Shemini Atzeret   The Eighth Day of Assembly   שְׁמִינִי עֲצֶרֶת

The eighth day of Sukkot. In places where Sukkot has only
seven (7) days, it is combined with Simhat Torah. In the
Diaspora, it is celebrated the day after Hoshanah Rabbah.

MINOR FESTIVALS

During the Minor Festivals, the Jews can work.

<u>Hanukkah</u>   <u>Festival of Dedication</u>   חֲנֻכָּה

An eight-day festival starts on the 25 of Kislev in remembrance of the Jews' fight for religious freedom under Judah the Maccabee in 165 B.C.E. The eight days recall the miracle of the oil which was enough to burn for one day, but the oil lasted eight days. <u>See also</u>: Judah the Maccabee; Oil.

<u>Hanukkah</u>
Sides of "4" handshapes touch each other and then move away from each other in down arc movement. May wiggle the fingers to indicate the flame.
Palms facing oneself may be used.
Also sign for "Menorah".

<u>Menorah</u>   <u>Hanukkiyah [Modern Hebrew]</u>   חֲנוּכִּיָה

A nine-branched candlestick holder which represents the eight days of the miracle when the oil lasted in 165 B.C.E., and the ninth candle, <u>shammash</u>, which is used by a person to light the candle(s) each day of the eight days. See

"Sabbath" and "Modern Israel" for information on seven-branched menorah.

See also: Hanukkah; Shammash in "Sanctuary".

See Hanukkah above for sign.

Judah the Maccabee   Yehuda Ha-Makabee   יְהוּדָה הַמַכַּבִּי

In 165 B.C.E., he led the battle against the Syrians and Greeks and succeeded in getting them out of the land of Israel.

See also: Antiochus.

Antiochus   אַנְטִיוֹכוּס

The King of Syria from 175 - 164 B.C.E. who ordered the Jews to worship Zeus and defiled the Holy Temple.

Oil   Shemen   שֶׁמֶן

Oil is important in the story of Hanukkah and thus we eat food that is cooked in frying oil. Latkes [Y], Levivot (pl.) Levivah (s.): potato pancakes, traditional food from Eastern Europe, and Sufganiyot: jelly-filled doughnuts, traditional food in Israel are cooked in oil. Note: In Hebrew, each letter has a number. If any word has a similar number as another word, they are considered to be divinely related. In this case, shemen has 390 and the word for eight, shemonah, has 395, showing another reason for the tradition.

Dreidel [Y]   Sevivon   סְבִיבוֹן

A four-sided top used in game that is played during Hanukkah. Each side has a Hebrew letter...

    Nun -- nothing   נ

    Gimel -- take all   ג

    Hay -- take half   ה

    Shin -- put in.   ש

These Hebrew letters together stand for the saying "Nes gadol hayah sham." which means "A great miracle happened there."

Dreidel
Thumb and index finger rub together on top of the opposite palm as if turning a small top on it.

Gelt [Y]   Money   געלט

In honor of the child who was said to have found the jar of oil, children are given a few coins as presents on Hanukkah.

Tu B´Shevat   Jewish Arbor Day   טוּ בִּשְׁבָט

The 15th day of the month of Shevat, a special day to plant trees in Israel; "The New Year of the Trees."

Purim   Feast of Lots   פּוּרִים

A holiday on the 14th day of Adar, in remembrance of Queen Esther who saved the Jews in Persia by pointing out Haman as the traitor to the King. The story is told in the Book of Esther. It is also in remembrance of the rescue from destruction of the Jewish religion.

See also: Queen Esther; King Ahasuerus; Haman.

Purim
Double "K" handshapes at the corners of the eyes move out to "U" handshapes.
Other variation:
"P" handshape in one-hand "Celebrate" movement.

Queen Esther   Ester Ha-Malkah   אֶסְתֵּר הַמַּלְכָּה

Became the queen and wife of King Ahasuerus after Vashti. She stopped the King from listening to Haman who wanted to kill all the Jews. She was raised by Mordecai, her cousin or uncle.

See also: King Ahasuerus; Haman; Mordecai.

See next page for illustration.

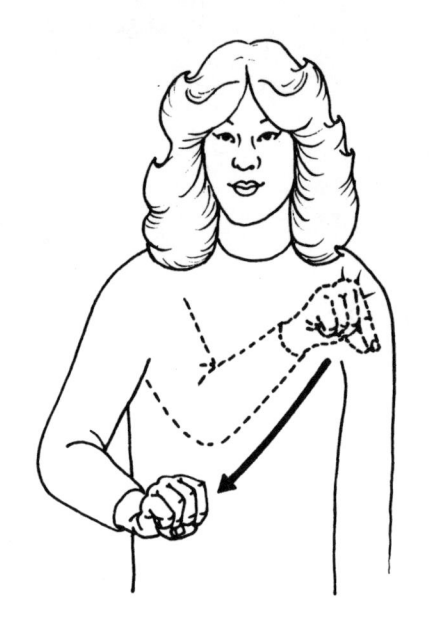

Queen Esther
"Q" handshape at the opposite shoulder moves diagonally down into "E" handshape to waist.
Other variation:
May use "E" alone in the same movement as above.

Mordecai   Mordehai   מָרְדְּכַי

A cousin or uncle who brought up Esther. He was King Ahasuerus' doorkeeper. Haman plotted to have him hung but at the end of the story, it was Haman who was hung instead.
See also: Queen Esther; Haman.

King Ahasuerus   Ahashverosh   אֲחַשְׁוֵרוֹשׁ

The King of Persia who took Esther as his queen after the death of his first queen, Vashti, and who had agreed to Haman's plan to kill all the Jews in Persia.
See also: Queen Esther; Haman; Vashti.

Vashti   וַשְׁתִּי

A Persian Queen who refused to attend the banquet with her husband and was punished by death.
See also: King Ahasuerus.

Haman   הָמָן

A prime minister of Persia and a favorite of King Ahasuerus and who had planned to destroy all the Jews in Persia. He was hanged for this.

See also: Purim; King Ahasuerus.

Grogger   Ra´ashan   רַעֲשָׁן

A noisemaker used whenever Haman´s name is mentioned during the reading of the Book of Esther, so to "wipe-out" the name of Haman.

Grogger
Thumb on "X" index finger in space near the face in circular movement. May add "Noise" sign.
Clue: 1-handed "Celebrate" movement.

Hamantaschen [Y]   Haman´s Pockets   המן־טאשן

A triangle-shaped pastry filled with poppy seed or prunes traditionally served on Purim.

See next page for illustration.

Hamantaschen
Open "G" handshapes with index fingers and thumbs touching move out to closed "G" handshapes slightly forming triangle-shape.

Megillah   Scroll   מְגִילָה

A megillah is a scroll with one roller whereas the Torah scroll has two rollers.

Megillah
Start with double "A" handshapes touching, then one hand moves out in slight waving movement.
Other variation:
"Purim" + "Story".

Shushan Purim   שׁוּשַׁן פּוּרִים

According to the Megillah, all cities surrounded by walls celebrate Purim one day late. Today only Jerusalem does.

Matanot Le´Evyonim   מַתָּנוֹת לָאֶבְיוֹנִים

Gifts given to the poor on Purim.

Mishloah Manot   Shaloch Mones [Y]   מִשְׁלֹחַ מָנוֹת

Exchange of gifts of fruits and nuts to friends on Purim.

Day of Holocaust   Yom Ha-Shoah   יוֹם הַשּׁוֹאָה

A day in remembrance of six million Jews who were annihilated by the Nazis during World War II. Marked on the 27th day of the month of Nisan, it is the anniversary of the Warsaw Ghetto revolt.

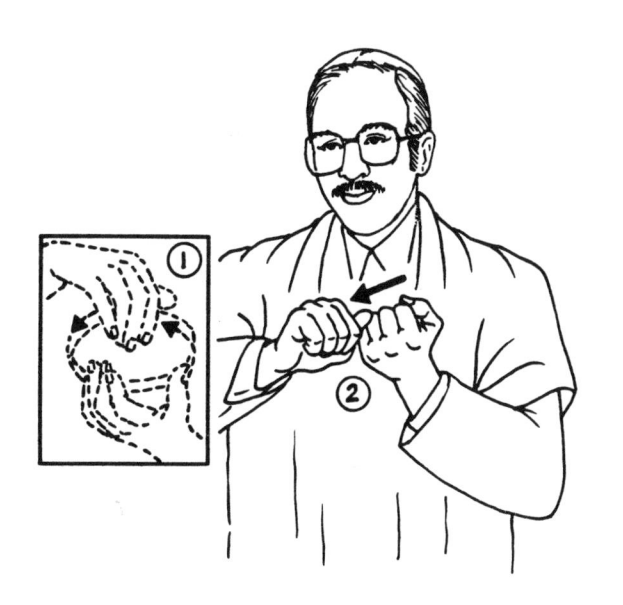

Holocaust
1. "Confuse" movement, then
2. "Destroy" movement.
Other variations:
"Terrible" + "Destroy".
"Destroy" + "Jewish".

Israel Independence Day   Yom Ha-Atzmaut   יוֹם הָעַצְמָאוּת

On May 14, 1948, Israel became a nation by the act of the United Nations. It is celebrated on the 5th day of the month of Iyyar.

See also: State of Israel.

Lag B´Omer   לַ"ג בָּעוֹמֶר

A minor holiday which takes place on the 33rd day of the 49 days between Passover and Shavuot in remembrance of the time when the Jews, pretending to shoot bows and arrows, studied in the woods to hide from the Romans who had forbidden the teaching of Judaism. It is a favorite holiday for children in Israel because bonfires are lit in the evening. This is also the anniversary of the death of Rabbi Simeon Ben Yohai, the alleged author of the Zohar. On this day many religious children receive their first haircuts. Furthermore, this holiday suspends the semi-mourning period of the counting of the omer (Sefirat Ha-Omer) between Passover and Shavuot.

See also: Zohar.

Lag B'Omer   Israel Version
1. "S" handshape behind "S" handshape.
2. Dominant "S" moves toward own body changing into tight "8" handshape, then
3. changes into "4" handshape while the passive "S" moves forward in space.
Clue: Bow and arrow.

Tisha B´Av   Ninth Day of Av   תִּשְׁעָה בְּאָב

Ninth day of month of Av in remembrance of the day when the First and Second Temples in Jerusalem were destroyed.

General Terms Used in Holidays

Fast   Tzom   צום

As mentioned in Yom Kippur; it is also applied by observant Jews to other holidays such as Tisha B´Av; Taanit Esther; Tzom Gedaliah and Asarah Betevet. Some Ultra-Orthodox Jews fast every Monday and Thursday as they believe that is an act of self-control and it brings them to a higher spiritual level. There are different perspectives on fasting. Some are to sensitize to the plight of the poor and to suppress our animal instincts to be purely spiritual.

Happy Holiday   Hag Sameah   Gut Yontuff [Y]
                 חַג שָׂמֵחַ   גוט יום טוב

Hol Ha-Mo´ed   חול המועד

Intermediate days of a Festival or Holiday between the first and last days of Passover and Sukkot. These are the days in which people may work, spend money, etc., but keep the holiday mood. These are, also, the days when some Jews do not use the phylacteries.

Holiday   Yom Tov   יוֹם טוֹב

A festival day.

Mahzor   מַחֲזוֹר

A special prayer book for the Holidays.

See also: Siddur; Mahzor in "General Ritual Objects"

Rosh Hodesh   רֹאשׁ חֹדֶשׁ

Beginning of the Jewish month or new moon. Now is a half-day holiday in Israel.

Rosh Hodesh
"New" + "Moon".

JEWISH LIFE

This chapter focuses on the Jewish life from Aggadah to Zionism. It includes signs that were developed in the 1982 NCJD Convention Workshop. Customs and traditions are emphasized in this chapter.

Interestingly, the sign FRUM, which traditionally means Orthodox or a really religious person was rejected by the sign language users as the one not within the concept of Judaism and the American Sign Language. However, when Rabbi Ebstein brought to the author's attention that the sign is FRUM is valid, it suddenly regains its rightful position in the book.

Aggadah (Aramaic)   אַגָּדָה

Stories and parables passed on by word of mouth from generation to generation.

See also: Haggadah; Talmud.

Averah   Sin   עֲבֵרָה

See Mitzvah; Sin.

Baal Teshuvah   Penitent   בַּעַל תְּשׁוּבָה

The one who repents for his sins; is considered on higher spiritual level than the one who never sinned (Tzaddik). The one who has accepted strict Orthodox teachings of the Hasidic movement.

Before Common Era (B.C.E.); Common Era (C.E.)

These are used in dates instead of "Before Christ" (B.C) and "Anno Domini" (In the Year of Our Lord; A.D.). They refer to the same time (B.C.E. is before the year "0" and C.E. is after the year "0").

BRANCHES OF JUDAISM

Judaism is based on Torah, God and Israel.

Orthodox   Dati   דָּתִי

Orthodox Judaism maintains the traditional laws of the Bible strictly as interpreted and developed by the rabbis in the Talmundic days. In other words, they believe every word in the Torah came from God to Moses and all later statements by the rabbis are also the word of God. They observe all the mitzvot or commandments strictly, including Sabbath and dietary laws.

See also: Moses; Ten Commandments; Halakhah; Dietary Laws.

Orthodox Variation 1
"O" handshape in space in front moves back and forth sideways.
Orthodox Variation 2 (Insert)
"O" handshape against the opposite palm facing up moves outward. These signs were developed at 1982 NCJD Convention Workshop.

<u>Frum [Y]</u>   <u>Dati</u>   <u>Pious</u>   דָּתִי

Strictly religious - strictly following the Jewish law.

<u>Frum</u>
"F" handshape on the opposite palm moves across and out. A traditional sign for "Orthodox" or "Very religious person".

<u>Hasidim</u>   <u>Hasidut</u>   חֲסִידוּת   חֲסִידִים

A movement in Eastern Europe which began in the 18th century. They believed that God is reached through song and dance and mystical prayer; studied the Kabbalah. Founded by the Baal Shem Tov. Today they are considered Ultra Orthodox Jews. <u>See also</u>: Kabbalah.

Kapotah [Y] —③   קאפאטע

A long, silky outer garment worn by some Hasidic men.

Payess [Y] —②   Payot (pl.)   Payah (s.)   פֵּיאוֹת

The sidecurls by the ears worn by some males. The Biblical Commandment says that the farmers have to leave a "corner" of their fields alone as it belongs to God. Comparatively, the Rabbis stated that the corners of the face are God's and must be left alone.

Shtreimel [Y] —①   שטריימל

A fur-trimmed hat worn by some Hasidic men.

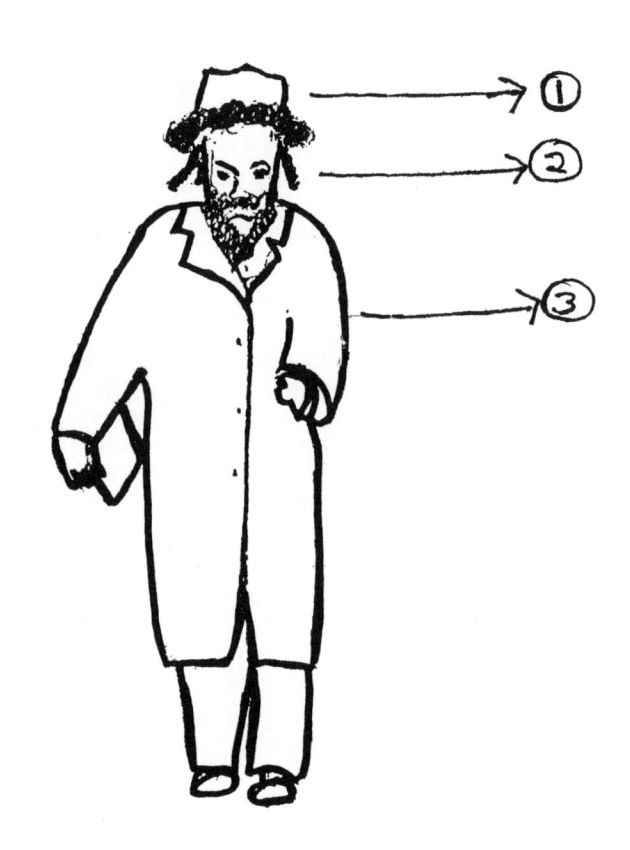

Sheitl [Y] שייטל

A wig worn by some Orthodox women after marriage. The belief is that exposing a woman's real hair in public is not modest.

Conservative

The movement seeks to conserve those elements of the historical Jewish experience which unify the Jewish people. Therefore, it is concerned with the continuity of Jewish law, practice, and common Jewish experiences. It seeks to interpret the past in the light of modern understandings of Jewish history and destiny. This movement began in the 19th century in Europe but grew in the United States. Solomon Schechter was the founder.

See also: Ten Commandments; Moses; Halakhah; Dietary Laws; Torah; Minyan.

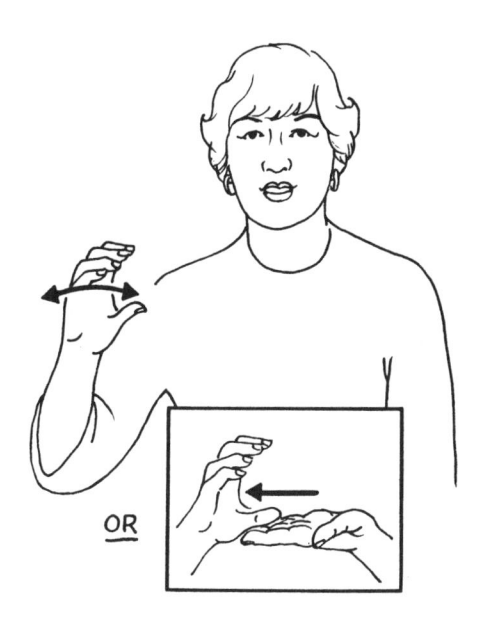

Conservative Variation 1
"C" handshape in space in front moves back and forth sideways.
Conservative Variation 2 (Insert)
"C" handshape on opposite palm facing up moves outward.
These signs were developed at 1982 NCJD Convention Workshop.

Reconstructionism

Reconstructionism, the fourth major movement in Judaism, originated from the writings of Rabbi Mordecai Kaplan in the 1930's. Reconstructionists maintain that Judaism is an evolving religious civilization. They assert that Jewish religion must change and grow to be meaningful to Jews today. But Judaism is more than simply a religious way of life and can only be understood within a civilizational context.

See also: Reform; Orthodox.

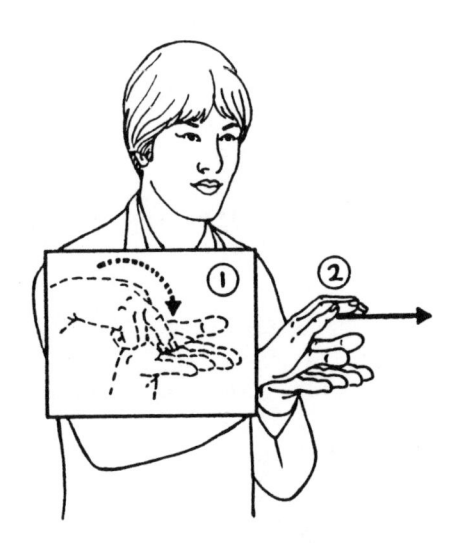

Reconstructionism
1. Tips of "R" handshape touch the opposite palm, then
2. change to "C" handshape moving straight out.
This sign was developed at 1982 NCJD Convention Workshop.

Reform

This movement began in Germany and spread to the United States by the middle of the nineteenth century. Rabbi Isaac Meyer Wise was the most important builder of Reform Judaism in America. In America Reform Judaism has stood for: the equality of men and women, the acceptance of prayer in English as well as Hebrew, a liberal approach to Jewish laws and customs, and a prophetic concern for social justice. Reform Judaism embraces Zionism, and it recognizes the freedom and responsibility of each Jew to make intelligent choices for Jewish living.

See also: Halakhah; Dietary Laws; Ten Commandments; Moses.

Reform   Variation 1
"R" handshape in space moves back and forth sideways.
Reform   Variation 2 (Insert)
"R" handshape on opposite palm facing up moves outward.
These signs were developed at 1982 NCJD Convention Workshop.

Hov, Hovah   חוֹב, חוֹבָה

Duty, obligation, e.g. ten percent (10%) of earnings for the Tzedakah.

See also: Tzedakah.

Codes of Jewish Law

Because Jews have been studying, interpreting and creating new legal decisions for over 2,000 years, it was necessary to create books to organize all these laws. One rabbi who did so was Moses Maimonides (Rambam). His code, the <u>Mishneh Torah</u>, was written in the 12th century. Another major code is the <u>Shulkhan Arukh</u>, written by Joseph Caro in the 16th century.

    They were codified into four volumes:

    I   Daily life; Shabbat; Holidays - <u>Orah Hayyim</u>

    II   Kashrut (Kosher food); Conversion - <u>Yoreh Dayah</u>

    III Marriage and Divorce - <u>Even Ha-Ezer</u>

    IV   Civil and Business Law - <u>Hoshen Mishpat</u>

<u>See also</u>: Torah; Talmud; Ten Commandments.

Halakhah

הֲלָכָה

The laws that are in the Torah are called the Written Law. they are the foundation of all Jewish Law. After the Torah was written, new laws developed which each generation <u>told</u> the next generation. They are called the Oral Law. The Written Law and the Oral Law together are called Halakhah -- Jewish Law.

    <u>See also</u>: Torah; Talmud; Ten Commandments; Moses; Reform; Orthodox; Conservative; Codes of Jewish Law.

Talmud תַּלְמוּד

The Talmud is a collection of Jewish knowledge which was passed from generation to generation. It is also known as the Oral Law. The Talmud has two parts. First, it is the Mishnah, which is a collection of Jewish Law, compiled before 200 C.E. Second, are the arguments and discussion of the Rabbis about these Laws. That part is called Gemarah. The Talmud does not have only Jewish Law (Halakhah). It also contains legends, tales and wise sayings (Aggadah). There are actually two Talmuds. The Talmud of the Jews of Israel (the Yerushalmi) and the Talmud of the Jews of Babylon (the Bavli). Though the Mishnah is the same, the Gemarahs are different.

See also: Haggadah; Aggadah; Halakhah; Torah.

Kabbalah   Tradition   קַבָּלָה

The collection of mystical Jewish prayers, poems, and texts. Kabbalah influenced Hasidic thought about God, and the nature of humanity and the world.

See also: Hasidism; Zohar.

Zohar   זֹהַר

A part of the Kabbalah in which most teachings are based on Jewish mysticism. The Hasidim consider it to be as holy as the Bible and the Talmud.

See also: Kabbalah; Lag B´Omer.

Conversion

See Mikveh.

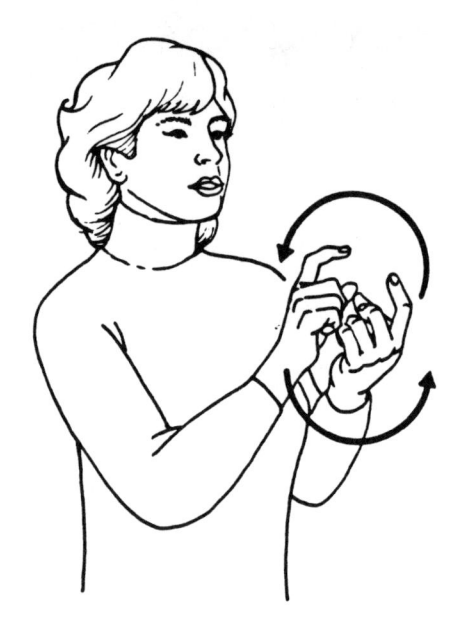

Conversion
"X" handshapes touching each other move in turning movement.
Clue: "Change" movement.
Other Variation:
Use the same movement as above with "C" handshapes.

Custom   Minhag   מִנְהָג

Religious customs are less strict than formal religious laws, but are recognized by the Talmud. E.g., the wearing of the yarmulka by the Orthodox men is a very strong custom - not law.

See also: Halakhah.

Sign for CUSTOM is found in other excellent sign language resource books.

Dietary Laws   Kashrut   Food Fit for Jewish Eating   כַּשְׁרוּת

Define the laws in regard to preparing and keeping food; not permitting the eating both dairy (milchik) and meat (fleishig) in the same meal; the way the animals are killed; eating certain foods while not permitting others.

Dairy   Milchik [Y]   מילכיק

Foods that have any dairy product, which are not permitted to be eaten with meat.

See also: meat (fleishig).

Kosher   Kasher   Kashrut   כָּשֵׁר, כַּשְׁרוּת

What is permissible to eat according to the Dietary Laws.

    Kosher Le-Pesah -- fit for Passover use.   כָּשֵׁר לְפֶּסַח

    Glatt [Y] -- very strictly kosher. (Refers only to meat.)   גלאַט

    Basar Kosher [Y] -- kasher the meat which means sprinkling coarse salt on kosher meat ritually slaughtered, and soaking to drain off the blood.

    See next page for illustration.   בָּשָׂר כָּשֵׁר

Note: Ashkenzazic way of pronouncing "Kasher" is "Kosher".

See also: Dietary Laws.

Kosher Variation 1
"K" handshape on the opposite palm at wrist moves across and out.

Kosher Variation 2
"K" handshape in space moves back and forth.

Meat   Fleishig [Y]   פלײשיק

Flesh of animals that have cloven hoof and chew their cud. Not permitted to be eaten with dairy.

See also: Dietary Laws; Dairy.

Sign for MEAT is found in other excellent sign language resource books.

Parve   פאַרעווע

Foods that have no meat or dairy products in them. E.g., eggs, fruits, fish and vegetables. They may be eaten with either meat or dairy.

See also: Meat; Dairy; Dietary laws.

Traif [Y]   Forbidden Food   Terefah   טרייף

Food that is forbidden to be eaten according to the Dietary Laws.

Bodek   בּוֹדֵק

The one who examines an animal that is slaughtered to determine if it is pure and edible. If the killing is done by the bodek, he is called shohet u´vodek (ritual slaughterer/examiner).
See also: Shohet.

Hekhsher   הֶכְשֵׁר

The symbol of approval by proper Rabbis that the food is Kosher. The symbol may be K or Ⓤ or Ⓚ stamped on package.

Mashgiah   מַשְׁגִיחַ

A religious supervisor at hotels, restaurants, food packaging plants, caterers and butchers to make sure the food strictly follows the Dietary Laws.
See also: Dietary Laws.

Shohet   שׁוֹחֵט

An observant Jew who knows the traditional way of slaughtering an animal (Shehitah) in order to minimize the suffering of the animal. He is certified by the rabbi to perform this ritual.

Gematria גִּימַטְרִיָּה

A method developed by Jewish Talmudic scholars of adding up the numerical values of all the Hebrew letters in a word and using the total as a means of interpreting the text. They would see a relationship between words that add up alike.
See Hebrew Alphabet in Appendix for numerical values.

Hanukkat Ha-Bayit חֲנוּכַּת הַבַּיִת

Dedication of (new) house or home by putting a mezzuzah on the doorpost. See Mezzuzah in "General Ritual Objects".

Heritage

Status acquired by birthright.

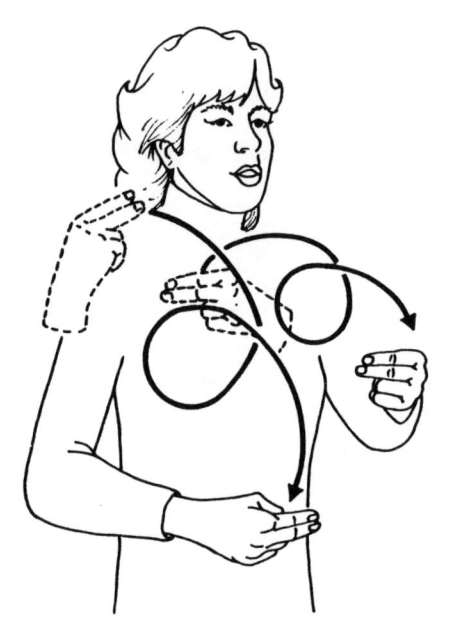

Heritage
"H" handshapes circle each other while moving downward from the shoulder.

Jewry, Judaism   Yahadut   Yiddishkeit [Y]   יַהֲדוּת

A faith or a concept based on One-God belief (monotheism) and culture, history and other related matters.

See also: Jew(s); Jewish; Judah; Hebrews.

Sign: "Jews" + "Group".

Jew(s); Jewish   Yehudim (pl.); Yehudi (m.); Yehudiah (f.)

יְהוּדִי, יְהוּדִיָה

Members of the Jewish people or of the Jewish faith; descended from the Semitic race.

See also: Jews in "Biblical and Historical Jewish Personalities"; Hebrews; Israelites; Judah/Judea; Hebrew (Languages); and Semites.

Kaddish   קַדִישׁ

A general prayer for praising God. It does not mention death.

See also: Kaddish in "Life Cycles".

Kiddush   קִדוּשׁ

A blessing usually in the form of wine. It symbolizes the expression of happiness at being Jews; having holidays and for having Sabbaths.

See also: Kiddush in "Sabbath"; Kabbalat Shabbat.

Life   Hayyim   (Hai: shortened form)   חַיִים

The Torah and the Talmud teach that life is very important. Torah is considered "tree of life". In Hebrew, letters have numerical value. The value of chai is 18. In toasting,

"L´chayim" is said which means "To life".

See also: Gematria.

Life
"L" handshapes move straight upwards along the chest from the waist.

Midrash   מִדְרָשׁ

A short story or explanation which attempts to fill in the gaps or answer puzzling questions found in the Bible.

Mikveh   מִקְוֶה

A ritual bath for the purpose of purification and cleanliness of the body. A religious woman immerses in it after her menstruation; before a wedding and after childbirth. A religious man takes it every Friday and the day before each Festival. The actual immersion is called "tevilah" in Hebrew. It can also be used for conversion purposes.

See next page for illustration.

Mikveh
1. and 2. "Holy"
3. "Bath".

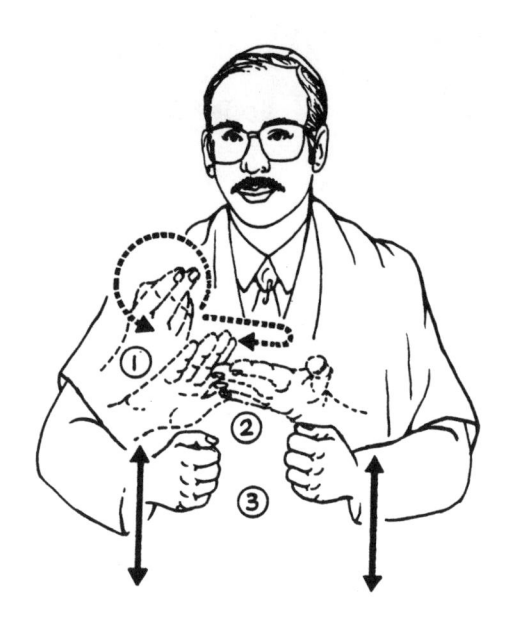

Minyan   מִנְיָן

A quorum of ten males and/or females over age 13 is necessary to begin (1) the community prayer; (2) the recital of Kaddish; and/or (3) the reading of the Torah. Orthodox Judaism includes males only.

See also: Minyan in "Sanctuary".

Minyan
Soft "M" handshapes circle as in group movement. May add "10" sign after "M" movement.
Clue: Group of people.

85

Mitzvah   Divine Commandment   מִצְוָה

A deed, whether it is a moral or a ritual act, is done in the sense of "joining together with God and person". An opposite of Averah.

See also: Averah; Mitzvot.

Religion; Religious

Expression of person's belief in superhuman power; godly; pious.

Religion; Religious
"R" handshape from the heart moves out in space.
See traditional sign "Frum" as other variation.

Ritual

Form or order in conducting a religious ceremony.

See next page for illustration.

Ritual
"R" handshape moves slightly down on top of the opposite fist.

Seminary

A theological school for training rabbis, cantors and Jewish educators, and advanced and intensive study of the Torah.
See also: Yeshivah.

Seminary
"S" handshape against opposite palm facing up moves up in arc movement.

Semites

The Bible says the Semites are the descendants of Noah's son, Shem. They are Hebrews, Arabs, Phoenicians, Babylonians and Assyrians. Today's Jews are of mixed races. Hebrew, Arabic and Aramaic languages are the Semite languages. Anti-Semites by today's usage means a hatred of the Jewish people.

Simhah   שִׂמְחָה

Rejoicing; celebration.

Tradition

Passing down from generation to generation, especially by oral communication.

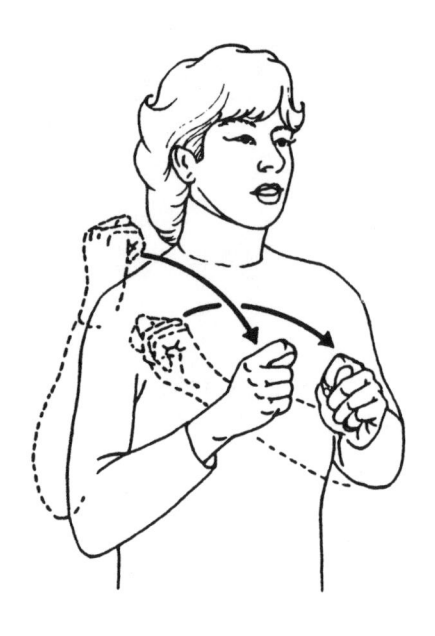

LEFT
Tradition Variation 1
"T" handshapes circle each other while moving downward from the shoulder.

RIGHT
Tradition Variation 2
"T" handshape moves down on top of the opposite "T" handshape.
Other Variation:
Use the same movement as above but on the top of the "S" handshape.

Ashkenazim   אַשְׁכְּנַזִים

The Jews from Central and Eastern Europe. Their everyday language was Yiddish. They used Hebrew for praying.

<u>Some customs</u>: Naming child after a deceased person; tombstones stand up; the Torah is lifted up and shown <u>after</u> the reading of the Torah.

<u>See also</u>: Sephardim; Yiddish.

Sephardim   סְפָרַדִים

The Jews who came from Spain, Portugal and other areas surrounding the Mediterranean Sea. Ladino is their everyday language while Hebrew is their Holy tongue. Their pronunciation of Hebrew is different from those of Ashkenzim. Today in Israel, Sephardic Hebrew is spoken. In Israel Sephardim includes Jews from the Middle Eastern countries.

<u>Some customs</u>: Naming a new baby after a living person; flat tombstones; the Torah is lifted and shown <u>before</u> the reading of the Torah.

<u>See also</u>: Ladino; Ashkenazim.

Tzedakah   צְדָקָה

Righteous acts or deeds including charity. All Jews are expected to give to those less fortunate than they so to help make the world better. A tzadik is a person who performs righteous acts or deeds.

See also: Hov, Hovah.

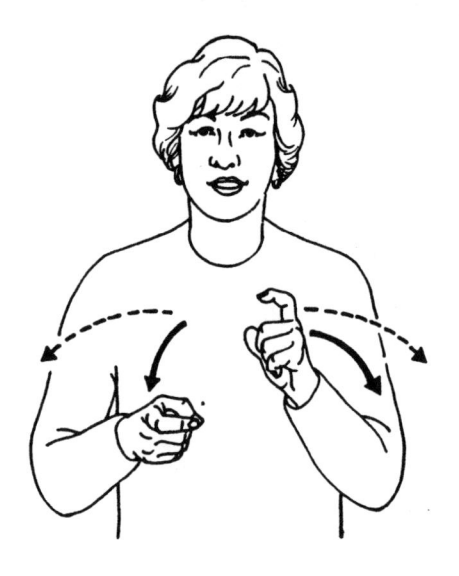

Tzedakah
Double "X" handshapes move outwardly in alternating movement.
Other variation:
"Donation" + "Equal".

Yeshiva   Yeshivah   יְשִׁיבָה

An academy where the students receive Jewish and Hebrew education, and study the Torah. In some yeshivot, the students are ordained as rabbis.

See also: Seminary.

See next page for illustration.

Yeshiva
"Y" handshape against the opposite palm moves upward in arc movement.

Zionism

An idealistic concept in which Israel is the homeland for the Jews. Zion is the poetic name for the land of Israel. The concept was founded by Theodore Herzl at the end of the 19th century.

LANGUAGES

In Biblical history, the Semite languages were Aramaic and Hebrew. Ladino evolved from Spanish mixed with Hebrew. Yiddish is a Germanic language full of words borrowed from Hebrew, Polish, Russian and other Slav languages. Favorite Yiddish expressions are found in the chapter, "Yiddish Expressions".

Aramaic

An early language of the Jewish people closely related to Hebrew language. The Kol Nidre and Kaddish prayers, Ketubah, Get and most parts of the Talmud are written in Aramaic.

Hebrew   Ivrit   עִבְרִית

A Semitic language of the Bible and Modern Israel. The Holy Tongue (Leshon Ha-Kodesh); used for prayers, worship and Jewish scholarship.

See sign gloss for Jew(ish), Hebrew, Israel, in "Biblical and Historical Jewish Personalities".

Ladino

Evolved from Spanish, written in Hebrew characters, and sprinkled liberally with Hebrew words. Spanish mixed with Hebrew used in daily spoken language by Sephardic Jews.

See also: Sephardim.

<u>Yiddish</u>

Germanic language written in Hebrew characters and full of borrowed words from Hebrew, Polish, Russian, etc. Spoken by Ashkenazic Jews.

<u>See also</u>: Ashkenazim.

LIFE CYCLES

Life Cycles focuses on words and signs from birth to death. Again, signs for some words may be found in other sign language resource books.

Shalom Zakhar   שָׁלוֹם זָכָר

A celebration on Friday night after the birth of a boy.

Berit Milah; Bris [Y]   Circumcision   בְּרִית מִילָה

A ceremony in which the foreskin covering a penis is removed on the eighth day after the birth. This is a tradition in which a covenant is made with God in the same way as Abraham's agreement with God. The boy is given his Hebrew and English name during the ceremony.

Brit
Right thumb in "cutting" movement around the left thumb.

Circumcision

See Berit Milah.

Elijah's Chair   Keesay Eliyahu   כִּסֵא אֵלִיָהוּ

A chair on which the sandek sits while holding the baby during the berit milah.

See also: Sandek

Mohel   מוֹהֵל

A Jewish person trained and specialized in performing berit milah.

Naming

See Berit Milah and Simhat Bat.

Sandek   סַנְדָק

The person holding the baby during the berit milah, usually the child's grandfather or godfather.

Se'udat Mitzvah   סְעוּדַת מִצְוָה

The festive meal celebrating a religious occasion such as a circumcision, wedding or bar/bat mitzvah. It is considered a religious duty.

Simhat Bat　שִׂמְחַת בַּת

A ceremony in which female babies are welcomed into the covenant between the Jewish people and God, usually done within the first 30 days after birth. At the ceremony, the Hebrew and English name is given to the baby girl. Baby girls are also named during the reading of the Torah after her birth.

Pidyon Ha-Ben　　Redemption of the First Born　פִּדְיוֹן הַבֵּן

Thirty days after a first-born son is born, a celebration takes place where the parents symbolically "buy back" their son from God. This is in remembrance of the deliverance of the Israelite firstborn sons when the Egyptians' sons were slain just before the Exodus; only for the Israelites - not for Kohanim or Levites.

See also: Exodus.

Bar/Bat Mitzvah　　Benai Mitzvah　בַּר/בַּת מִצְוָה　בְּנֵי מִצְוָה

An event in which a boy or girl at the age of 13 is expected to assume the full responsibilities in religious duties; for own actions and is also given full adult privileges in the tradition. He/she is called upon to read the Torah at the Sabbath services. This kind of celebration was not known in the Biblical history.

See next page for illustration.

Bar/Bat Mitzvah
One hand in soft "A" handshape in winding motion around the opposite hand or forearm twice. For girl--add "Girl" sign before or after the sign. Also a sign for "Tefillin".

Haftarah הַפְטָרָה

A reading from the Prophets after the Torah reading in which boy or girl reads as a part of their bar/bat mitzvah ceremony.

See also: Haftarah in "Vocabulary for Prayer".

Confirmation

The Reform and Conservative Jews have this service usually at the age of 16 or 17 when they come and state their commitment to learning of Judaism.

See next page for illustration.

Confirmation
Double bent closed "5" handshapes with thumbs and index fingers touching downward at the top of the head pat twice.

Engagement   Erusin (Aramaic)   אֵירוּסִין

An engagement period before marriage.

Sign for ENGAGEMENT is found in other sign language books.

Tena´im   תְּנָאִים

Terms of engagement agreement.

Marriage   Kiddushin   קִידוּשִׁין

Legal union of a man and woman as husband and wife.

Sign for MARRIAGE is found in other sign language books.

    Bride   Kallah   כַּלָה

    A woman who is about to be married.

Sign for BRIDE is found in other sign language books.

Groom   Hatan   חָתָן

A man who is about to be married.

Canopy   Huppah   חֻפָּה

Held or hung over the bride and groom at the wedding and is considered a symbol of the new home for the couple.

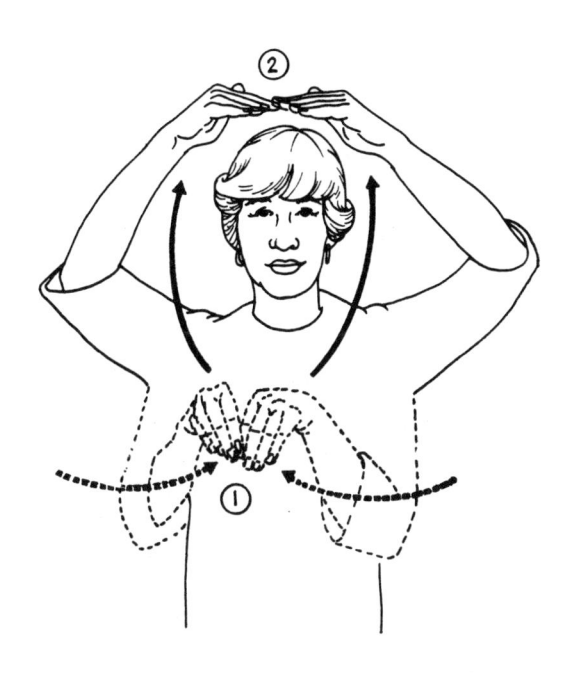

Canopy Variation 1
1. "Wedding" sign
2. Move up to overhead into closed "5" handshapes fingers touching.

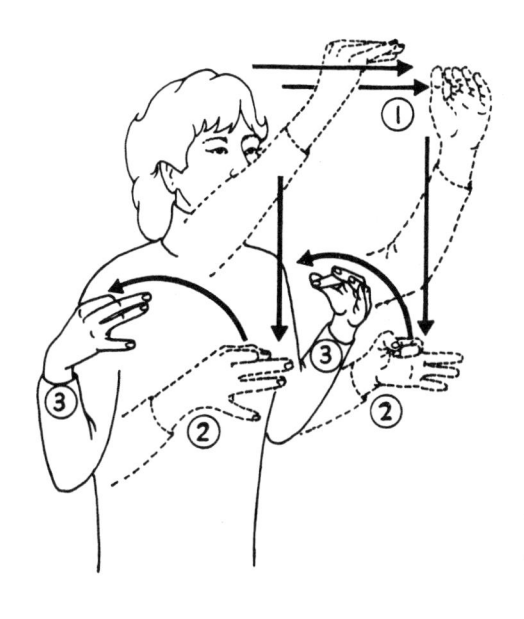

Canopy Israel Version
1. Bent, closed "5" handshapes overhead, palms down move forward, then
2. change to "F" handshapes, palms facing each other, then
3. move backward.
Clue: Canopy overhead with four poles.

Breaking the Glass

The groom stamps on wrapped drinking glass at the wedding ceremony symbolizing the remembrance of the destruction of Jerusalem, and fragility of love.

Bringing in the Bride   Hakhnassat Kallah   הַכְנָסַת כַּלָּה

An old custom which helps a poor or penniless girl to get married with the provision of clothes, furniture and household utensils. This is done in secret so that the bride does not know who gives them to her.

Dowry   Nedunyah   Naden [Y]   נְדוּנְיָה

In Biblical days, the groom paid the bride's father a price (mohar). Traditionally, the father of the bride provides a dowry. If the bride was poor, the community provided. . .not practiced in most cases except among Hasidim.
See also: Bringing in the Bride.

Nissu´in (Aramaic)   נִשּׂוּאִין

In Biblical times, it was the consummation of the marriage under the huppah.

Wedding Contract   Ketubah   כְּתוּבָּה

A wedding contract written in Aramaic which lists the groom's responsibilities, and the bride's promises. Today, modern Jews use them to symbolize wedding vows as well as the legal contract.

Sheva Broches [Y]; Sheva Berakhot   Seven Blessings
שֶׁבַע בְּרָכוֹת

The seven blessings are recited during the ceremony and immediately after the wedding by the wedding guests each day for one week.

Mikveh   Ritual Bath   מִקְוֶה

See Mikveh in "Jewish Life".

Mazel Tov   מַזָל טוֹב

Congratulations! "Ad me´ah ve´esrim!" -- "Life to 120 years!"

Divorce; Divorce Certificate   Get   גֵט

A marriage is dissolved with a document written in Aramaic. According to Talmud, it is possible for a man to divorce against the wife´s will. For modern Jews, it is done with both spouses´ agreement.

Sign for DIVORCE is found in other excellent sign language books.

Cemetery   Bet Hayyim or Bet Olam   בֵית חַיִים, בֵית עַלְמִין

A burial place. The graves of close relatives are visited on the anniversary of the death and before the High Holy Days.

Sign for CEMETERY is found in other sign language books.

Kaddish   קַדִיש

A prayer in Aramaic which praises God; said in memory of the dead; reminds us that God is with us in death as in life.

See also: Kaddish in "Jewish Life".

Sign: "Mourn" + "Prayer".

Keri´ah   קְרִיעָה

In the past, and in Orthodox custom, tearing clothes was a sign of mourning. Today, a ribbon is provided which is cut as a symbol that our heart is torn.

Mourning   Avelut   אֲבֵלוּת

During the shivah, a mourner´s candle burns in the home of the mourner. It burns for seven days. A one-day candle is used on yahrzeit and Yom Kippur.

<u>See also</u>: Yahrzeit.

Sign for MOURNING is found in other sign language books.

Sheloshim   שְׁלֹשִׁים

A 30-day mourning after the burial of a close relative observed by some Jews.

Shivah   Seven-day Mourning   שִׁבְעָה

Traditionally, the mourners sit on low stools without shoes; mirrors may be covered. Food is brought in by friends and relatives. A special candle that burns for seven days is lit and the kaddish is recited. No leather is worn.

<u>See also</u>: Kaddish; Mourning.

See next page for illustration.

Shivah
"U" handshapes overlap each other in "Sitting" movement.
Other variations:
Sign "Mourn" before or after "Shivah".
Sign "Week" before or after "Shivah".
"Wooden Seat" + "Seven Days" + "Mourn".

Shroud   Tahrihin   תַּכְרִיכִים

A white Jewish burial garment. A deceased male is usually covered with his own tallit and buried in it.

Unveiling

Usually before the first anniversary of the death; a tombstone is dedicated at the grave.

Yahrzeit [Y]   Anniversary of Death   יאָרצייט

According to the Hebrew calendar, a 24-hour candle is lit at home and Kaddish is recited in the synagogue. A contribution to charity can be made in memory of the deceased on this day.
Sign: "Memory" + "Annual" + "Dead".

Yizkor   יִזְכּוֹר

A memorial service for the deceased on Passover, Shavuot, Sukkot and Yom Kippur.

<u>Sign</u>: "Service" + "Memory" + "Dead".

MODERN ISRAEL

This chapter focuses on selected words and signs related to today's Israel. Related information on ancient Israel is found in chapters on Personalities and History. In order to maintain Israel's own signs, the signs for Arab, Eilat, Haifa, Jerusalem and Tel Aviv are borrowed from Israel.

Aliyah   Going Up   עֲלִיָה

Moving to Israel and becoming an Israeli resident. The concept of "going up" comes from the physical necessity of going up to Jerusalem which is located on a series of hills, while "going down" means to Egypt.
See other version of Aliyah in "Sanctuary".

Arab

Semitic people said to be the descendants of Ishmael. Today they are mostly Moslems and live in the Middle East.
See also: Ishmael.

Baal Teshuvah

Soviet Jews who have emigrated to Israel are able to observe Jewish religious laws and customs - very often for the first time in their lives.
See also: Baal Teshuvah in "Jewish Life".

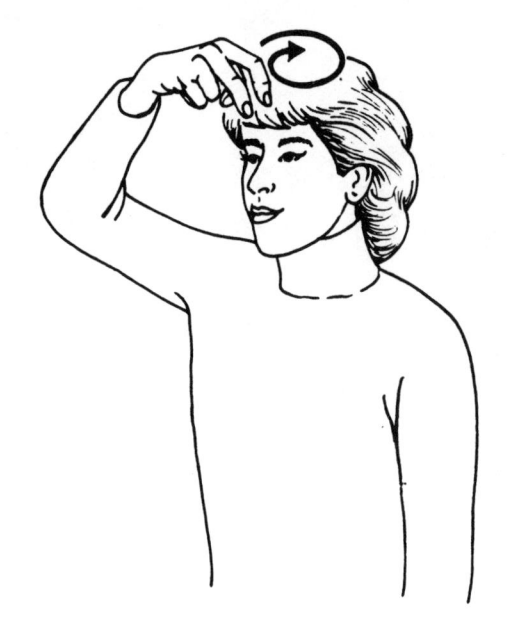

Arab   Israel Version
Bent "V" handshape moves in a circle over the top of the head representing the Arab headband.
Other variation:
Using "A" handshape, follow the similar movement as above.

Diaspora (Greek)   Scattering   Galut   גָּלוּת

Galut means forced scattering or exile. In history, the Jews had many exiles. Following the destruction of the First Temple, the Babylonian Exile took place. After the Second Temple was destroyed, the Jews were exiled among the Roman Empire.

See also: Tefutsot; Galut.

See next page for illustration.

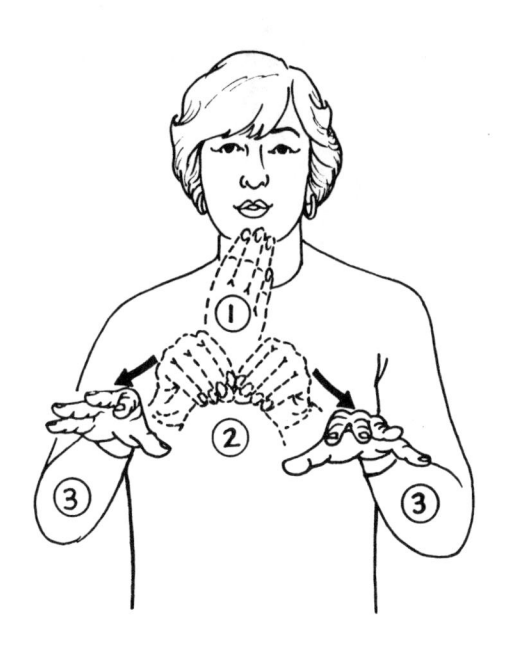

Diaspora
1. "Jew" on chin, then
2. Flat "O" handshapes with index fingers and thumbs touching, then
3. Move and spread out in space in slightly bent open "5" handshapes.

Eilat   אֵילַת

A seaport on the Southern Part of Israel.

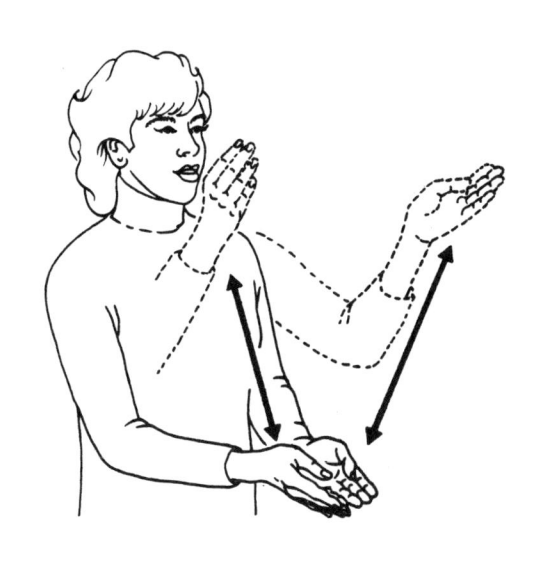

Eilat Israel Version
Closed "B" handshapes, palms facing each other, move downward to below the waist, touching at the little finger edges.

Falafel פַלָפֶל

Fried, ground chickpeas stuffed in pita bread which is a popular food in Israel today.

Haifa חֵיפָה

A seaport at the foot of Mount Carmel in Israel.

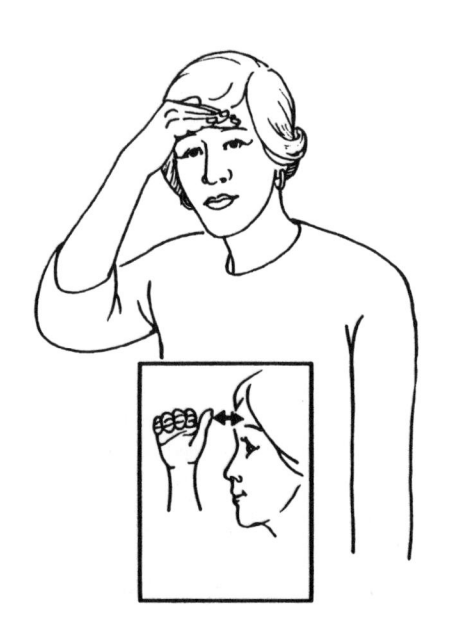

Haifa Israel Version
Bent closed "5" handshape thumb side taps on the forehead twice.
Clue: Looking far away; view from Mount Carmel.

Halutzim (pl.); Halutz (s.)   Pioneer(s) חֲלוּצִים

Pioneers in Palestine which includes all the early settlers of many groups with the goal of establishing a Jewish national homeland, both physically and spiritually.

Hatikvah   Hope   הַתִּקְנָה

Israeli National Anthem written by Naftali Imber, the poet. Words can be found in Songs.

Horah   הוֹרָה

A traditional Israeli dance in which the basic formation is a circle. One of the popular dances at the Jewish celebrations.
Sign: "Israel" + "Dance".

Israel   יִשְׂרָאֵל

See State of Israel, below.
See sign gloss on Israel in "Biblical and Historical Jewish Personalities" and "Biblical and Jewish Places and History".

Israeli(s)   Yisra´elim (pl.)   Yisra´eli (m.); Yisra´elit (f.)

יִשְׂרָאֵלִי, יִשְׂרָאֵלִית

A citizen of Israel; also called Israelite.
See also: Sabra.

Jerusalem   Yerushalayim   יְרוּשָׁלַיִם

The capital of Israel.
See Jerusalem in "Jewish History".

Kibbutzim (pl.); Kibbutz (s.)   Collective Farm   קִבּוּץ

A communal settlement whose members own everything jointly; mostly agricultural, but may be industrial. They dedicated themselves to the concept of Zionism and the establishment of Israel was due, in part, to their efforts.

See also: Zionism.

Knesset   כְּנֶסֶת

The Israeli Parliament. Established in 1949, composed of several political parties, located in Jerusalem.

Sign: "Israel" + "Government".

Menorah   מְנוֹרָה

In Israel - seven branched candelabrum, which is a symbol for the State of Israel.

See also: "Hanukkah" and "Sabbath" for other ´Menorah´.

Moving to Israel

See Aliyah in this chapter.

Sabra   צָבָּר

Native-born Israeli.

See also: State of Israel.

State of Israel   Medinat Yisrael   מְדִינַת יִשְׂרָאֵל

The Modern State of Israel formed by the United Nations´ charter in 1948 to create it as a homeland for the Jewish people.

See also: Israel in "Jewish Personalities"; "Jewish History"; Children of Israel.

Tel Aviv   תֵּל־אָבִיב

The largest city in Israel.

Tel Aviv   Israel Version
Open "G" handshape at the corner
of an eye moves out closing "G"
handshape.
Clue: Sign like "Eyeglasses".

Tefutsot   Diaspora   תְּפוּצוֹת

Hebrew word for Diaspora. There is a museum in Tel Aviv about
the Diaspora which is called Bet Ha-Tefutsot.

PRAYER VOCABULARY

This chapter deals with the words and signs traditionally used during the prayer services from Adonoi to Zion. There are cross references on text and sign illustrations/gloss; sign gloss with the illustrations; words for which signs may be found in other sign language resource books, and no signs borrowed from Israel. This chapter also includes general blessings/prayers, and songs. For Psalm 23, see Appendix.

Adonai
See God for various Hebrew words.

Amen   אָמֵן
Response to blessing or prayer in which God´s name is mentioned ("I agree" or "So be it") at the end of the blessing or prayer which another person says.

Amidah   Standing Silent Prayer   עֲמִידָה
Eighteen Benedictions said on weekdays. Also called Shemoneh Esreh - Reciting while standing.   שְׁמוֹנֶה־עֶשְׂרֵה

For the list of 18 Benedictions, see Appendix.

    See next page for illustration.

Anahnu Korim   אֲנַחְנוּ כּוֹרְעִים
Reciting while bending knees.

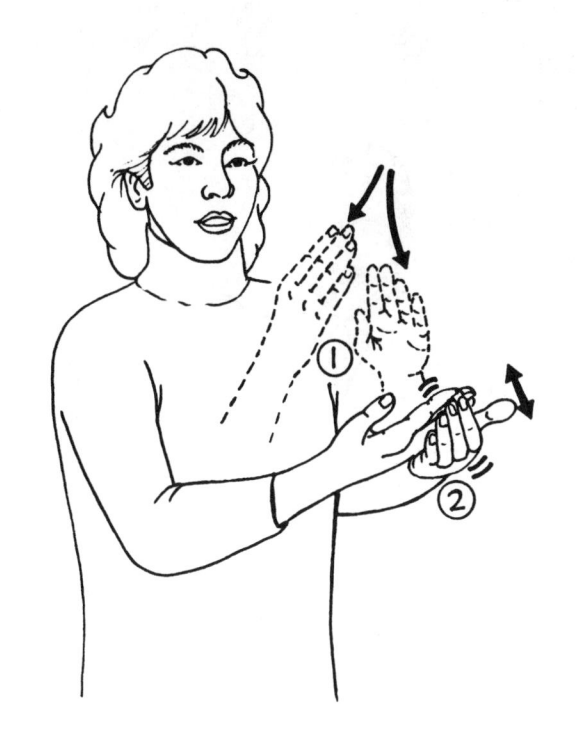

Amidah
"Silent" + "Pray".
See "Pray" in "Vocabulary".

Ark of the Covenant   Aron Ha-Berit   אֲרוֹן הַבְּרִית

See in "Biblical and Jewish History".

Barekhu   בָּרְכוּ

First words in prayer opening the main part of the service.
See Blessed, below.

Benediction   Berakhah   Blessing   בְּרָכָה

Also means "Praise" - part of the daily ritual.

Bible

Holy Scriptures; Torah.

See also: Torah in "Sanctuary"; Holy Scriptures in Appendix.

See Bible in "Sanctuary".

See next page for illustration.

Bible Variation 1
"Holy" + "Book".

Bible Variation 2
"B" handshape taps twice against the opposite palm facing against the "B" handshape.
Clue: "Constitution" movement.

Blessed

    Blessed art Thou - <u>Barukh Attah</u>.　בָּרוּךְ אַתָּה

    Blessed (Praised) is the Lord Our God - <u>Barukh Attah</u>

       <u>Adonai Elohenu</u>.　בָּרוּךְ אַתָּה יְהוָֹה אֱלֹהֵינוּ

<u>See also</u>: Benediction; Lord.

See next page for illustration.

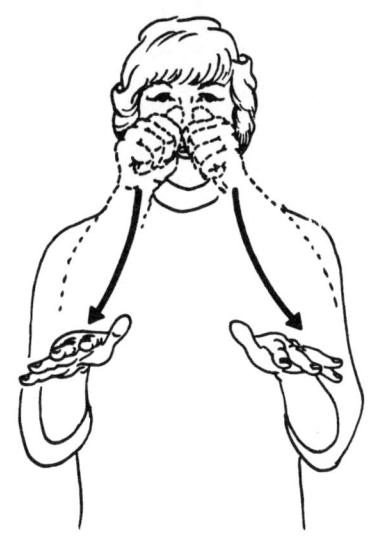

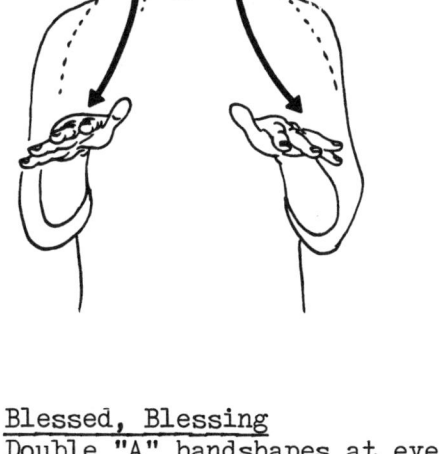

Blessed, Blessing
Double "A" handshapes at eye level move down opening into "5" handshapes.
Other variation:
Same handshapes start from mouth and move down using the above movements.

Art Thou
In connection with "Blessed" index finger at lips, then moves into closed "5" handshape palm facing up.

Blessings

    Blessing of the Candles - <u>Birkat</u> <u>Ha-Nerot</u>   בִּרְכַּת הַנֵּרוֹת

    Blessing after the Meals - <u>Birkat</u> <u>Ha-Mazon</u>   בִּרְכַּת הַמָּזוֹן

    Blessing of the Torah - <u>Birkhot</u> <u>Ha-Torah</u>   בִּרְכוֹת קְרִיאַת הַתּוֹרָה

    Blessing before the Meals - <u>Ha-Motzi</u>   בִּרְכַּת הַמּוֹצִיא

Children of Israel   Benai Yisra´el   בְּנֵי יִשְׂרָאֵל

See in "Biblical and Jewish Personalities".

Consecrate   Kadesh   קַדֵשׁ

Sanctify - make holy; set aside; make special.

See also: Sanctify.

Sign: "Make" + "Holy" or "Clean".

Covenant   Berit   בְּרִית

An agreement between a person and God.

See Berit Milah in "Life Cycles".

Covenant
1. Index finger at forehead; other index finger in space;
2. Dominant finger moves down to meet parallel with the other index finger in space;
3. then sign "Relate" upward to Heaven.
Other variation;
Sign "Agree".

Eternity

Everlasting; infinity.

Father   Melekh   מֶלֶךְ

Our Father; our King - Avinu Malkenu   אָבִינוּ מַלְכֵּנוּ

Father of Mercy - Av Ha-Rahamim   אַב הָרַחֲמִים

See also: God.

Five Books of Moses

See Pentateuch in "Sanctuary".

Fruit of the Vine   Peree Ha-Gafen   פְּרִי הַגֶּפֶן

Represents wine.

God   Elohim   אֱלֹהִים

    God Almighty - El Shaddai   אֵל שַׁדַּי

    God Most High - El Elyon   אֵל עֶלְיוֹן

    Eternal God - Adon Olam   אֲדוֹן עוֹלָם

    The Lord our God - Adonai Elohenu   אֲדֹנָי אֱלֹהֵינוּ

    The Name (of God) - Ha-Shem   הַשֵּׁם, ה׳

    God willing - Im yirtseh Ha-Shem   אִם יִרְצֶה ה׳

    Thank God! - Barukh Ha-Shem!   בָּרוּךְ ה׳

God
"B" handshape in front of the forehead moves lateral up and down in arc movement.

Haftarah   הַפְטָרָה

Reading from the Prophets after the Torah reading.

See Haftarah in "Life Cycles".

Halleluyah   הַלְלוּיָה

Praise God!; Praise with joy.

Halleluyah
"Praise" + "Celebrate".

Hear O Israel   Shema Yisrael   שְׁמַע יִשְׂרָאֵל

Declaration of unity of God.

Heaven   Shamayim   שָׁמַיִם

Sign can be found in other sign language resource books.

Holy; Holiness   Kedushah   קָדוֹשׁ, קְדוּשָׁה

Holy
"H" handshape moves in "2" movement, then across the opposite palm.
Other variation:
"H" handshape into closed "5" handshape across the opposite palm as in "Clean" sign.

Israel   Yisra´el   יִשְׂרָאֵל

See also: Israel in "Biblical and Jewish History"; "Biblical and Jewish Personalities".

King   Melekh; Melakhim (pl.)   מֶלֶךְ, מְלָכִים

King of the Universe, Ruler of the Universe - Melekh Ha-Olam.

We have no King but You. - En Lanu Melekh Ela Attah.

Life   Hayyim   חַיִּים

See Life in "Jewish Life".

Lord   Adonai   אֲדֹנָי

    The Lord is One - <u>Adonai</u> <u>Ehad</u>.   אֲדֹנָי אֶחָד

    The Lord is Our God - <u>Adonai</u> <u>Elohenu</u>.   אֲדֹנָי אֱלֹהֵינוּ

    My Lord - <u>Adonai</u>.

Lord
At the opposite shoulder, "L" handshape moves out and up as to Heaven.
Other variation:
"L" handshape at the opposite shoulder moves diagonally down to the waist.

Meditate

Pray by oneself.

Messiah   Mashiah   מָשִׁיחַ

See in "Biblical and Jewish Personalities".

Mishebayrakh   מִי שֶׁבֵּרַךְ

A special prayer which asks God to send health to the sick.

Mitzvot (pl.)   Commandments   מִצְווֹת

There are 613 mitzvot in the Torah. These are the rules which tell us how to act spiritually, morally, physically and ethically.

See also: Mitzvah.

Pentateuch   חוּמָשׁ

Five books of Moses.

See also: Bible in "Sanctuary" and in Appendix.

Praise   Hallel   הַלֵּל

    Praise the Lord, to whom our praise is due -

        Barekhu et Adonai Ha-Mevorakh.

    Praise the Lord, to whom praise is due now and forever -

        Barukh Adonai Ha-Mevorakh Le-Olam Va´ed.

Pray

See Prayer in "Sanctuary".

      See next page for illustration.

Repent

See Yom Kippur in "Holidays" for sign gloss.

      See next page for illustration.

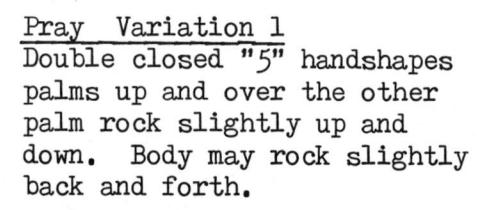

Pray   Variation 1
Double closed "5" handshapes palms up and over the other palm rock slightly up and down. Body may rock slightly back and forth.

Pray, Worship   Variation 2
Hand covering the other hand move inward in small circular movements.

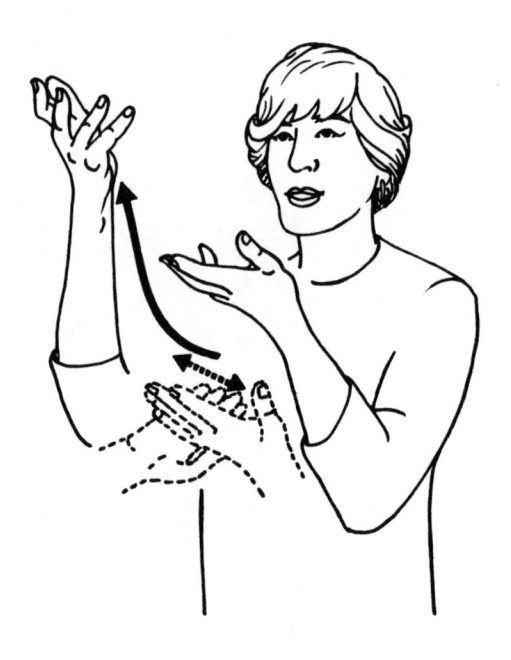

Repent
"Clean" + "Offer" upward.
Other variations:
-"Sorry".
-See Yom Kippur for "Repent" variation.

Ritual

See Ritual in "Jewish Life".

Rock

Strength (symbolizing God).

Sacrifice

See Sacrifice in "Biblical and Jewish History"; Abraham.

Sacrifice
"Offer" in upward movement.

Sanctify   Le-Kadesh   לְקַדֵּשׁ, קָדֵשׁ

See also: Consecrate; Kiddush.

Shalom   שָׁלוֹם

Peace; greetings; hello; goodbye; love.

Peace to you - Shalom Aleikhem.

Sign: PEACE or HELLO or GOODBYE or LOVE.

Sin   Hayt   חֵטְא

Not following the teachings and laws of God.

Sin
Double index fingers pointing each other in front of own body move out in circular movements twice.

Soul   Neshamah   נְשָׁמָה

Spirit.

Soul
"F" handshape at heart moves wavingly up while the passive "F" handshape remains at heart.
Other variation:
Double "F" handshapes index and thumb fingers touching, then top "F" handshape moves up with palm down.

Ten Commandments   עֲשֶׂרֶת הַדְּבָרוֹת

Given to Moses by God on Mount Sinai during his 40 years wandering. The Ten Commandments are listed in the Appendix. See also: Moses; Mount Sinai.

Ten Commandments
"10" handshape shakes back and forth, then "C" handshape taps on the opposite palm on fingers, then moves down and taps at bottom of the palm.
Clue: "Constitution" movement.

Thee, Thou, Thine   Attah   אַתָּה

Thee
Straight or slightly closed "5" handshape moves slightly upward as to heaven, palm toward self.
Thou
Index finger points up in air.
Thine
Palm toward heaven using the same movement as "Thee".

Torah תּוֹרָה

See Torah in "Sanctuary".

Torah
Two "A" handshapes with palms facing each other roll out as if unwinding the scrolls.
Other variations:
May use "C" or "T" handshapes in similar motion as above.
May add raising the hands up as if lifting the Torah.

Universe   Olam עוֹלָם

Master (King) of the Universe - Ribono Shel Olam.
רִבּוֹנוֹ שֶׁל עוֹלָם

Universe
"U" handshapes in "World" movement.

Zion   Tzeyon   צִיוֹן

The poetic name for the Land of Israel and Jerusalem.

See also: Zionism.

GENERAL BLESSINGS/PRAYERS

Food:

Bread, Hallah and Matzah

Blessed art Thou, the Lord Our God, Ruler of the Universe who takes bread out from the earth.

Barukh Attah Adonai, Elohenu Melekh Ha-Olam, Ha-Motzi Lehem Min Ha-Aretz.

Cake, Pastry and Pasta

Blessed art Thou ... Universe, Creator of the various sustaining foods.

Barukh Attah ... Borei Meenei Mezonot.

Vegetables from the Ground

Blessed art Thou ... Creator of the fruit of the ground.

Barukh Attah ... Borei Peree Ha-Adamah.

Fruits from Trees

Blessed art Thou ... Creator of the fruit of the tree.

Barukh Attah ... Borei Peree Ha-Etz.

Wine, Grape Juice

Blessed art Thou ... Creator of the fruit of the vine.

Barukh Attah ... Borei Peree Ha-Gafen.

Meat, Fish, Eggs, Drinks and Other Food

Blessed art Thou ... Universe, that everything comes into being at His bidding.

Barukh Attah ... Shehakol Nihyeh Bidevaro.

Kindling the Candles

Sabbath (Hanukkah, Yom Tov)

Blessed Art Thou, the Lord Our God, Ruler of the Universe, who made us holy with your Commandments and commanded us to light the Shabbat (Hanukkah, Yom Tov) candles.

<u>Barukh Attah Adonai, Elohenu Melekh Ha-Olam, Asher Kidshanu Be-Mitzvotav Ve-Tzivenu Lehadlik Ner Shel (Shabbat, Hanukkah, Yom Tov).</u>

Torah   תּוֹרָה

Before the Torah Reading...

Praise the Lord who is to be praised.

Praise the Lord who is to be praised forever and ever.

Praise be Thou, O Lord Our God, Ruler of the Universe, who chose us among all peoples and gave us the Torah.

Praise be Thou, giver of the Torah.

<u>Barekhu Et Adonai Ha-Mevorakh,</u>

<u>Barukh Adonai Ha-Mevorakh Le-Olam va-ed.</u>

<u>Barukh Attah Adonai Elohenu Melekh Ha-Olam, Asher Bahar Banu Mekol Ha Amim Ve-Natan Lanu Et Torato</u>

<u>Barukh Attah Adonai Noten Ha-Torah.</u>

After the Torah Reading...

Praise be Thou, O Lord Our God, Ruler of the Universe, who gave us the Torah of truth and planted within us eternal life.

Praise be Thou, O Lord, Giver of the Torah.

Barukh Attah Adonai Elohenu Melekh Ha-Olam Asher Natan Lanu Torat Emet, Ve-Hayay Olam Nata Betokhenu.

Barukh Attah Adonai Noten Ha-Torah.

Sheheheyanu שֶׁהֶחֱיָנוּ

Blessing for joyous events that do not take place every day; however, a Jew "makes Sheheheyanu" on the three major festivals which are: Passover, Sukkot and Shavuot.

Blessed art Thou, O Lord Our God, King of the Universe, who has kept us alive to this time.

Barukh Attah Adonai, Elohenu Melekh Ha-Olam, Sheheheyanu Ve-Kiyemanu Ve-Higiyanu La-Zeman Ha-Zeh.

Shema שְׁמַע

Hear O Israel! the Lord Our God, the Lord is One.

Shema Yisrael, Adonai Eloheynu, Adonai Ehad.

Barukh Shem Kevod Malekhuto Le-Olam Va´ed.

SONGS

My Dreidel

I have a little dreidel, I made it out of clay.
And when it's dry and ready. Then dreidel I shall play.
O Dreidel, dreidel, dreidel, I made it out of clay;
O Dreidel, dreidel, dreidel, Now dreidel I shall play.

It has a lovely body with leg so short and thin;
And when it is all tired, it drops and then I win.
O Dreidel, dreidel, dreidel, with leg so short and thin;
O Dreidel, dreidel, dreidel, it drops and then I win.

My driedel is always playful. It loves to dance and spin;
A happy game of dreidel. Come play, now let's begin.
O Dreidel, dreidel, dreidel. It loves to dance and spin.
O Dreidel, dreidel, dreidel. Come play, now let's begin.

Hatikvah - The Hope   (The National Anthem of Israel)

While ancient faith and yearning,
Within our bosoms dwell.
Still will be burning,
The hope of Israel.

                While Eastward with eyes glowing,
                Our hearts we turn in prayer.
                Our love will be flowing,
                To Zion waiting there.

None shall quench the hope of ancient years.
Hope that lives through sorrow and through tears.
This our salvation.
Israel shall be free and strong.

                Building a nation,
                In the land of David's song.
                In the land of David's song.

Rock of Ages

Rock of Ages, let our song
Praise Thy saving power;
Thou, amidst the raging foes,
Wast our shelt´ring tower.
Furious, they assailed us,
But Thine arm availed us,
And Thy word broke their sword
When our own strength failed us.

                                        Kindling new the holy lamps,
                                        Priests approved in suffering,
                                        Purified the nation´s shrine,
                                        Brought to God their offering.
                                        And His courts surrounding
                                        Hear, in joy abounding,
                                        Happy throngs singing songs
                                        With a mighty sounding.

Children of the martyr-race,
Whether free or fettered,
Wake the echoes of the songs
Where ye may be scattered.
Yours the message cheering,
That the time is nearing
Which will see all men free,
Tyrants disappearing.

Shalom

      Shalom . . . Shalom, you´ll find Shalom
          The nicest greeting you know.
It means Bonjour, Salute and Skoal and
        Twice as much as Hello.
It means a million lovely things,
          Like "Peace be yours" -- "Welcome Home"
And even when you say good-bye,
         If your voice has "I don´t want to go" in it,
Say goodbye with a little "Hello" in it.
        And say goodbye with
            SHALOM . . . SHALOM.

SABBATH

This chapter relates to Sabbath, per se. Other words/signs that are used or related to Sabbath services may be found in Sanctuary; Jewish Life; Vocabulary for Prayer and General Ritual Objects.

Sabbath   Shabbat   Shabbos [Y]   שַׁבָּת

Seventh day and the day of rest; a spiritual refreshment or restoration.

See also: Havdallah; Kabbalat Shabbat; Shomer Shabbat.

Sabbath   Variation 1
"F" handshape moves down in back of the opposite hand. (Erev Shabbat).

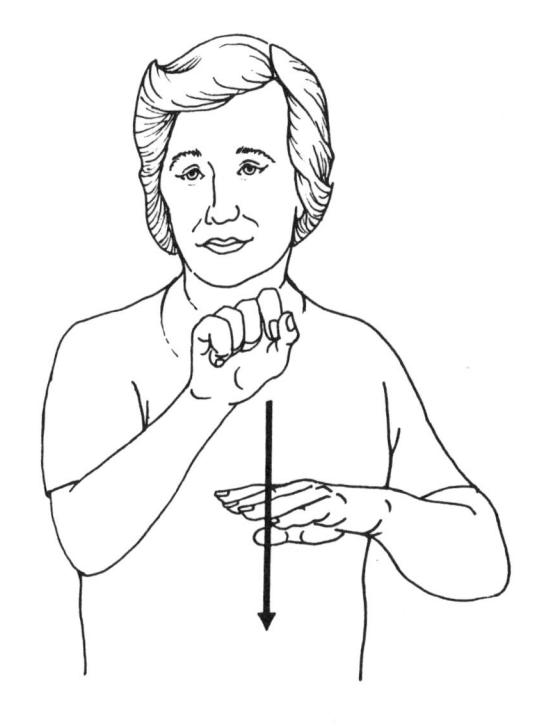

Sabbath   Variation 2
"S" handshape moves down in back of the opposite hand.
Other variation:
Sign "Saturday".

Besamim (Kufsat Besamim)   Spice Box   (קוּפְסַת) בְּשָׂמִים

A spice box, usually filled with cinnamon or cloves, used for blessing at Havdallah.

See also: Havdallah.

Hallah   חַלָּה

A braided or twisted bread traditionally eaten on Sabbath and the Festivals.

Ha-Motzi   הַמוֹצִיא

The blessing over the bread.

See Blessing in "General Blessings/Prayers".

Havdallah   הַבְדָלָה

A service ushering out the Sabbath. A braided candle which is lit at the sunset of the Sabbath, and spices are used. Havdallah separates the sacred from the secular. It parallels Kiddush which is used to bring in the Sabbath and other holy days.

See also: Kabbalah Shabbat; Kiddush.

See next page for illustration.

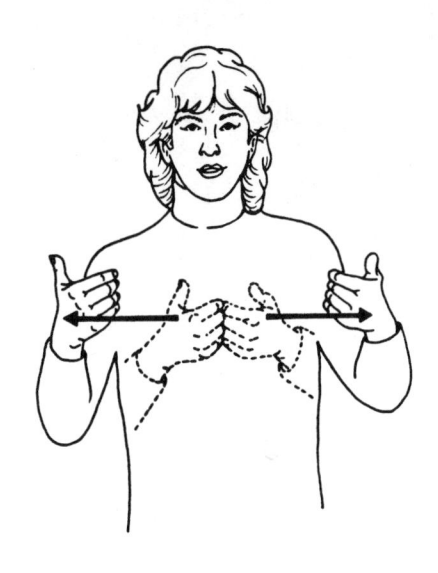

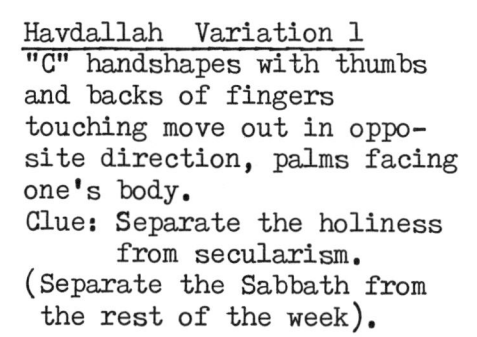

Havdallah Variation 1
"C" handshapes with thumbs and backs of fingers touching move out in opposite direction, palms facing one's body.
Clue: Separate the holiness from secularism.
(Separate the Sabbath from the rest of the week).

Havdallah Variation 2
"H" handshape moves down in arc outside the opposite arm with the "S" handshape.

Joy of the Sabbath

See <u>Oneg Shabbat</u> in this chapter.

Kabbalat Shabbat   Receiving Sabbath   קַבָּלַת שַׁבָּת

A service ushering in the Sabbath. At home after the Ma´ariv service, Kiddush is recited and lighting the candles takes place. Ha-Motzi is recited, too.

See also: Ha-Motzi; Kiddush; Lighting of the Candles; Havdallah.

Kiddush   קִדּוּשׁ

A blessing to sanctify Shabbat, Pesach, Rosh Hashanah, and other holidays. Wine is used to make the holiday special.
See also: Kabbalat Shabbat; Kiddush in "Jewish Life"; Havdallah.

Kindle

See Lighting of the Candles in this chapter.

Lighting of the Candles   Hadlakat Ha-Nerot   הַדְלָקַת נֵרוֹת

Light symbolizes the Torah and the person's soul. The candles are lit during a period of joy or sorrow.

- Shabbat - lit at the beginning of the Shabbat, usually two or more candles.
- Havdallah - lit at the end of the Sabbath using the braided candle.
- Ner Tamid - See "Sanctuary"
- Yahrzeit - See "Life Cycles"
- Menorah - For Sabbath, a candelabrum of two or more candles is used to usher in the Sabbath. See also: "Hanukkah".

Menuhah -- Shabbat rest.   מְנוּחָה

Oneg Shabbat   Joy of Sabbath   עֹנֶג שַׁבָּת

A celebration either on Friday night or Saturday afternoon with music or refreshments showing a joy of Sabbath.

<u>Pushke</u> [Y]   <u>Tzedakah Box</u>   פושקע

See <u>Pushke</u> in "General Ritual Objects".

<u>Shomer Shabbat</u>   שׁוֹמֵר שַׁבָּת

Strictly observing the Sabbath.

<u>Spice Box</u>

See Besamim.

SANCTUARY

This chapter focuses on things that are reverential, holy objects, and people in their relation to the religious service. There are some signs that are cross referenced as well as some signs that are in this chapter.

Aliyah   עֲלִיָה

Going up to Bimah to read from the Torah, or saying blessings before the reading.

See also: Aliyah in "Modern Israel".

Amidah   עֲמִידָה

Major prayer in service; said standing.

See also: Amidah in "Vocabulary"; list of Eighteen (18) Benedictions in Appendix.

Bible   Tanakh   תַּנַ"ךְ

Holy Scriptures; Five Books of Moses, Pentateuch.

See also: Pentateuch in "Vocabulary" and in Appendix.

Bimah   Pulpit   בִּימָה

An elevated platform in which the Torah is placed and read; also where the readers stand.

See next page for illustration.

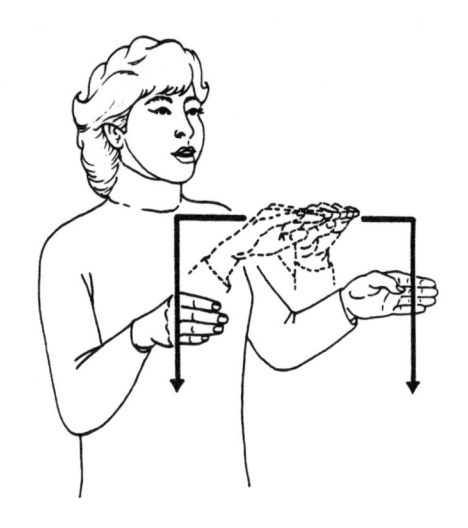

Bimah
Soft adjacent "B" hand-
shapes palms down, move
horizontally away from
each other, then turn so
that palms face each other
other and move dowards.

Breastplate   Tzitz   צִיץ

A silver shield hung over the Torah in the Ark. During the Holy
Temple days, it was worn by the High Priest.
See also: High Priest, Holy of Holies.

Cantor   Hazzan   חַזָן

A leader in the congregational singing; also, leads in certain
prayers as the emissary of the congregation.

See next page for illustration.

Cantor
"Sing", then closed "5" handshapes at each side of body move downward.
Other variation:
May add "Jewish" sign before or after the above movements.

Choir

An organized group of singers as opposed to the congregational singing.

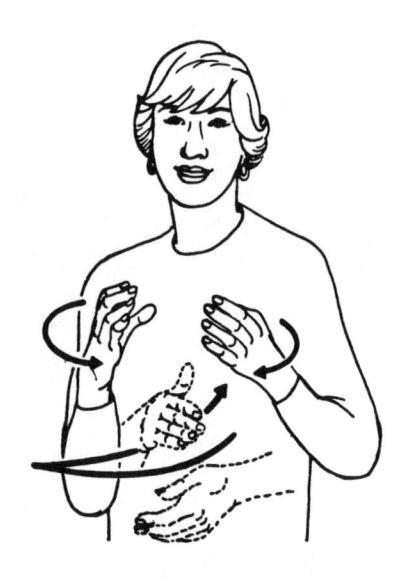

Choir
Bent closed "5" handshape above the opposite forearm swings back and forth, then change into soft "C" handshapes in "Group" sign movement.
Clue: Group singing.

Congregation

People attending the services at synagogues or temples.

Eternal Light   Ner Tamid   נֵר תָּמִיד

Hung in front of the Holy Ark (Aron Ha-Kodesh); traditionally is never extinguished. It symbolizes the presence of God.

Eternal Light
1. "Continue",
2. and 3. "Light".

Gelilah   גְּלִילָה

The honor of rolling up and dressing the Torah during the service.

Gentile

A person who is not Jewish.

Hagbah הַגְבָּהָה

The honor of lifting the Torah during the service.

Holy Ark   Aron Ha-Kodesh אֲרוֹן הַקֹּדֶשׁ

A cabinet in the center of the east wall of the synagogue where the Scrolls of the Torah are kept.

Holy Scriptures

See Bible; Old Testament.

Keter   Crown כֶּתֶר

A silver crown on top of the Torah; symbolizes: "Torah is a crown for Israel".

Kohen   Kohanim (pl.) כֹּהֵן (כֹּהֲנִים)

They are first in the Aliyah when it comes to reading the Torah; officiating at the Pidyon Ha-Ben and leading the priestly Benediction in the synagogues. See Kohen in "Biblical and Historical Personalities" for historical background.
See also: Pidyon Ha-Ben; Aliyah.

See next page for illustration.

Kohen
Double index and middle fingers together splitting in little and ring fingers together shape it "V" with index fingers and thumbs touching.

Mantle

After the Torah is wrapped or swaddled, it is encased in the mantle or sheath.

See also: Mappah.

Mappah   The Wrapper   מַפָּה

A wide sash used to tie around the scroll of the Torah.

Mehitzah   מְחִיצָה

A wall or barrier to separate men and women in Orthodox synagogues.

Menorah   מְנוֹרָה

See Menorah in "Holidays".

Minyan   מִנְיָן

A quorum of 10 or more persons needed to conduct public worship; recite the Kaddish and read the Torah. They must be above age 13, though a younger person can serve when a tenth person cannot be located.

See also: Minyan in "Jewish Life".

Ner Tamid - See Eternal Light.   נֵר תָּמִיד

Old Testament

Gentile name for the Jewish Bible whereas the Jews call it Holy Scriptures.

See also: Bible.

Parokhet   פָּרֹכֶת

A curtain over the Torah(s) in the Ark.

Pentateuch

See in "Vocabulary".

Prayer, Worship, Services   Daven [Y]   Tefilah   דאַוון

This tradition started back in the Biblical times when sacrifices took place. Now it is continued in the synagogue, home or other gathering place; recited in Hebrew or in English; offered regularly; Amidah is recited.

See also: Amidah.

See Pray in "Vocabulary".

Rabbi   Teacher   רַב, רַבִּי

This position was created in Talmudic times; ordained and competent to decide questions of Jewish law; spiritual leader of congregation, offers sermons; teaches and is a community-minded Jewish spokesperson.

Rabbi
"R" handshapes at sides of chest move straight down.
Clue: Wearing a tallit.

Rimmonim   Finials   רִמּוֹנִים

Separate decorative objects shaped like pomegranates adorning the tops of the rollers of the Torah. They symbolize great fertility and population increase in Israel.

Services

    Shaharit - Morning service   שַׁחֲרִית

    Minhah - Afternoon service   מִנְחָה

    Ma´ariv - Evening service   מַעֲרִיב

    Musaf - an additional service on certain Sabbath and holy
        days
                                                                      מוּסָף

See also: Patriarchs.

Shammash   Servant   שַׁמָּשׁ

The honorary custodian of the synagogue.

See Shammesh in "Hanukkah" for other definition.

Synagogue (Greek)   Bet Knesset   Shul [Y]   בֵּית כְּנֶסֶת

Three major functions:

    House of prayer - Bet Tefilah   בֵּית תְּפִילָה

    House of study - Bet Midrash   בֵּית מִדְרָשׁ

    House of assembly - Bet Knesset

Temple is the term used mostly by Reform Jews in referring to a synagogue.

Synagogue, Shul
"S" handshape taps on the back of the opposite hand.
Other variation:
"S-Y" handshape taps on the back of the opposite hand.

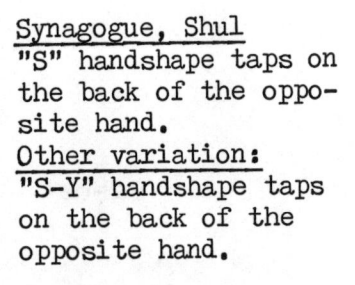

Temple
"T" handshape taps on the back of the opposite fist.

Talmud   תַּלְמוּד

See Talmud in "Jewish Life".

Torah   תּוֹרָה

Literally means "Teaching"; Five Books of Moses (Pentateuch).
Sefer Torah means the Scroll of Torah; Humash.
See also: Bible; Torah in "Vocabulary"; Pentateuch in Appendix.

Worship   Avodah

See Prayer.

Yad   יָד

A pointer used to read the Torah - usually in the shape of a pointed index finger; used to read the Torah because it is considered improper to touch the Torah with one´s finger as oil from the skin may damage the letters.

Yarmulka [Y]   Kippah   כִּפָּה   יַרמלקע

See Yarmulka in "General Ritual Objects".

TRADITIONAL JEWISH FOOD

If this book is to serve as a resource book to the Jewish Deaf Community, then the traditional Jewish food must be included. Though there are no illustrations in this chapter, other food illustrations may be found in sections on Passover and Purim. Again, some words with signs may be found in other sign language resource books.

Bagel

German word which means bracelet or ring; was considered as a protection against the forces of Evil Eye.

See also: Herring; Lox.

Bialy

A flat breakfast roll, sometimes sprinkled with onion; from Bialystok, Poland.

Blintz

Thin pancake, rolled around a filling which may be cheese, potato, or jams topped with sour cream or applesauce. If they are rolled and placed side by side, they suggest the tablet of the Ten Commandments.

See Shavuot in "Holidays".

Borscht

A Russian dish, mainly made with beets. May be eaten hot or cold.

Carp

Freshwater fish.

See Smoked Fish; Gefilte Fish.

Chicken

Traditional poultry eaten on the eve of Sabbath.

Chickpeas

One of the legumes, said to be associated with mourning in the Orthodox belief and a paradox to life itself; also served at Zehar celebration.

See Falafel in "Modern Israel".

Chopped Liver Gehakte Leber [Y]

Self explanatory.

Egg

A food of great contradiction; a reminder of joy mixed with sorrow.

See Seder Plate in "Holidays".

Egg Cream

A popular soda made with chocolate syrup, some milk and squirted with seltzer. (No, no egg is included.)

Farfel   Flekn   [Y]

Noodle dough cut to bits, then toasted, representing the misdeeds of past year done and over with; usually eaten at Passover.

Gefilte Fish

Prepared mainly with carp, pike or whitefish or all of them. According to Talmud, eating fish with bones in considered "work". Gefilte fish has no bones, so is suitable for Sabbath days; eaten in hope for better days to come.

Goulash

Cut up meat usually served on a bed of noodles.

Grieven

Fried chicken or goose skins.

Hallah

Sabbath egg bread, usually braided.

See Hallah in "Sabbath".

Halvah [Y]

A popular snack made from crushed sesame seeds and honey, originally from the Middle East.

Herring

May be eaten pickled or chopped; considered as a poor person's food.

See also: Bagel; Lox.

Honey

The main sweetener of the Jews for many years; represents sweetness. Israel is considered the land of "milk and honey".

See Rosh Hashanah in "Holidays".

Horseradish   Chrain [Y]

Grated horseradish root.

See Seder Plate in "Holidays".

Kasha   Mit Varnitchkes [Y]

Means cereal; actually is buckwheat groats, which is most popular eaten with bowtie noodles.

Kishke   Stuffed Derma

Meatless sausage put in a casing.

Knaidlach   Matzo Balls

Made with matzo meal, usually eaten with chicken soup at Passover and on the Sabbath.

Knish

A square or round dough with fillings ranging from chicken mixed with kasha, to pot cheese and pineapple, to mashed potatoes and fried onions. Slow cooking of the onions provides proper consistency for the filling. The secret of the dough is the use of gluten flour.

Kugel

A pudding or quiche-like casserole usually made with lokshen (noodles). Raisins, apples, cinnamon, or cheese may be added to lokshen. Other types of kugel may be farfel, kasha, potatoes or rice.

See Noodles.

Lox

Smoked salmon (belly or Nova Scotia); a very popular food item served with bagel and cream cheese. To the Jewish minds, the herring, a salty fish mentioned above, was considered food for poor people. Though maintaining the concept of eating salty fish, lox was considered a status symbol. Eaten with the bagel, it was also considered a protection against the Evil Eye. Could you imagine eating herring with bagel and cream cheese, or lox on white bread?

See also: Bagel; Herring.

Noodles   Lokshen   [Y]

Pasta made of eggs and flour. Available in different shapes, such as bowties, wide and flat, thin like spaghetti, alphabet shaped, and others. Best known noodle dish is the kugel.

Pike

Freshwater fish.

See Smoked Fish; Gefilte Fish.

Pomegranate

Represents romantic love and good health. Kabbalah says if the number of seeds in the fruit is 613, which is the number of mitzvot in the Torah, it is considered a perfect fruit. (Can you count them?)

Pumpernickel

Dark sourdough bread made from whole, coarsely ground rye flour.

Rye

A grain. The bread made with rye flour, usually a light bread, often with caraway seeds. This bread is usually good with cold cuts.

Schav

A cold soup made with sorrel or spinach usually eaten with a scoop of sour cream; typically eaten at Shavuot in honor of God's giving of the Ten Commandments to Moses at Mount Sinai. The green represents the grass at Mount Sinai.

Schmaltz [Y]

Fat from chicken or goose usually used in preparation of chopped liver or other typical dishes especially eaten with meat; not a dairy item.

Seltzer

A carbonated soda made with spring water. It was once bottled in siphonated bottles.

Smoked Fish

Usually carp, pike, or whitefish.

Sour Cream

Most popular served in many ways, e.g. with borscht, schav, blintzes, or mixed with fresh fruits.

Sponge Cake

Mainly made with eggs and cake meal; no yeast is used. Served during Passover.

Strudel

A pastry made with a thin sheet of rolled up dough, filled with fruit or cheese.

Stuffed Cabbage   Holoptsches [Y]

Much of nothing much, so to speak. Usually cabbage leaf rolled up and stuffed with ground beef mixed with rice.

Tzimmes [Y]

Usually eaten at Rosh Hashanah. Some forms of tzimmes may be any dried fruit with cinnamon and flour; potato; carrots or other food cooked slowly to blend the flavors. Mehren tzimmes (carrot tzimmes) are said to "assist in getting spiritual and economic good fortune" when eaten during the New Year (Rosh Hashanah).

Whitefish

Freshwater fish.

See Smoked Fish; Gefilte Fish.

YIDDISH EXPRESSIONS

Like traditional Jewish food, this book would not be complete without some favorite Yiddish expressions. There is a vocabulary of words to express shades of feeling.

Interestingly, in the past, Jewish women were never taught Hebrew, thus they spoke Yiddish to children who spoke it to their parents and then later to their own children.

Chutzpah............clever; wit; nerve

Feh!................Phew!; Ugh! phooey

Goy.................non-Jew

Greps...............burp

Gut Shabbes.........Good Sabbath

Gut Yontiff.........Good Holiday

Klupper.............slow worker

Klutz...............clod; slow-witted; graceless person

Kosher..............proper; correct; valid

Kvetch..............to whine

Macher..............doer

Maven..............."Know-it-all" (Note: not necessarily a pejorative.)

Mazel...............luck

Mensh or Mentch.....decent person

Meshugga............crazy

Metzia..............good find; bargain

Naches..............joy

Noodge	to pester
Nosh	little food; snack; eat, eat
Nu?	What's up?; So what?
Nudnik	pest; obnoxious person; nagger
Oy, oy vey	A short form for <u>Oy vey is mier</u> Vey--a German word for "Woe" Woe is me, Oh my!
Shalom Aleichem	Peace be with you
Shaygetz	non-Jewish man
Shikker	drunk
Shiska	non-Jewish woman
Shlemazel	A person who always has bad luck
Shlemeil	individual in an awkward situation
Shlepp	dragging
Shloomp	sloppy
Shmooze	unimportant or casual but not gossipy chatter
Shmutz	filth
Yente	gossipy; busybody
Zafti; zoftig	plump; almost fat
Zhlob	sloppy; clumsy; usually overweight

APPENDICES

TEN COMMANDMENTS   עֲשֶׂרֶת הַדִּבְּרוֹת

1. I am the Lord thy God.   אָנֹכִי ה׳
2. Thou shalt have no other gods before Me.   לֹא יִהְיֶה
3. Thou shalt not take the name of the Lord thy God in vain.   לֹא תִשָּׂא
4. Remember the Sabbath day to keep it holy.   זָכוֹר אֶת
5. Honor thy father and thy mother.   כַּבֵּד אֶת
6. Thou shalt not murder.   לֹא תִרְצָח
7. Thou shalt not commit adultery.   לֹא תִנְאָף
8. Thou shalt not steal.   לֹא תִגְנֹב
9. Thou shalt not bear false witness against thy neighbor.   לֹא תַעֲנֶה
10. Thou shalt not covet anything that belongs to thy neighbor.   לֹא תַחְמֹד

EIGHTEEN BENEDICTIONS   שְׁמוֹנֶה עֶשְׂרֵה

1. Patriarchs
2. God's power and resurrection of the dead
3. Sanctification of God's name
4. Wisdom and knowledge
5. Repentance
6. Forgiveness
7. Redemption
8. Healing
9. A good year
10. Gathering dispersed Israel
11. Justice
12. Action against wicked heretics
13. For the righteous
14. For Jerusalem
15. For Messiah of the House of David
16. For God's heartening to prayer
17. For God's acceptance of prayer
18. For thanks to God
19. For peace

(Some prayers are modified by Conservative and Reforms Jews.)

FINGERSPELLING USED IN ISRAEL

איות אצבעות ישראלי

אגודת החרשים בישראל
THE ASSOCIATION OF THE DEAF IN ISRAEL
Helen Keller Home, 13 Yad Labanim Blvd., Yad Eliahu, P.O.B. 9001, Tel. 31526

FINGERSPELLING USED IN ISRAEL

Key for Transliteration

Top Row
t; kh(h) or ch; z; o; v, w; h; d; g; v; b; a.

Middle Row
a (ayin); s; n (final); n; m (final); m; l; kh(h) (final); kh(h) or ch; k; i.

Bottom Row
t (th); s; sh; r; k; ts (final); ts; f (final); f; p.

Reprinted with permission from the Association of the Deaf in Israel.

HEBREW ALPHABET & GEMATRIA

LETTERS	TRANSLITERATION	NUMERICAL VALUE
א	Aleph	1
ב	Bet	2
ג	Gimel	3
ד	Daled	4
ה	Hay	5
ו	Vav	6
ז	Zayim	7
ח	Het	8
ט	Tet	9
י	Yod	10
כ	Caf	20
ל	Lamed	30
מ	Mem	40
נ	Nun	50
ס	Samech	60
ע	Ayin	70
פ	Pay	80
צ	Tsadi	90
ק	Kof	100
ר	Resh	200
שׁ	Shin	300
שׂ	Sin	300
ת	Tav	400

HEBREW MONTHS

Tishri..................September-October..... תִּשְׁרֵי ....

Heshvan.................October-November..... חֶשְׁוָן ....

Kislev..................November-December..... כִּסְלֵו ....

Teveth..................December-January..... טֵבֵת ....

Shevat..................January-February..... שְׁבָט ....

Adar....................February-March...... אֲדָר ....

Nisan...................March-April........ נִיסָן ....

Iyar....................April-May........ אִייָר ....

Sivan...................May-June......... סִיוָן ....

Tamuz...................June-July........ תַּמּוּז ....

Av......................July-August........ אָב ....

Elul....................August-September..... אֱלוּל ....

HOLIDAYS ACCORDING TO JEWISH YEAR

Rosh Hashanah..............1st of Tishri.........................

Yom Kippur.................10th of Tishri........................

Sukkot.....................15th of Tishri........................

Hanukkah...................25th of Kislev........................

Tu B´Shevat................15th of Shevat........................

Purim......................14th of Adar..........................

Passover...................15th of Nissan........................

Yom Ha-Sho´ah..............27th of Nissan........................

Israel Independence Day....5th of Iyyar..........................

Lag B´Omer.................18th of Iyyar.........................

Shavuot....................6th of Sivan..........................

Tisha B´Av.................9th of Av............................

PENTATEUCH

Genesis
Exodus
Leviticus
Numbers
Deuteronomy

PSALM

Psalm 23

The Lord is my Shepherd; I shall not want.
He maketh me to lie down in green pastures;
He leadth me beside the still waters.
He restoreth my soul.
He guideth me in straight paths for His name´s sake.
Yea, though I walk in the valley of the shadow of death,
I will fear no evil,
For Thou art with me;
Thy rod and Thy staff, they comfort me.
Thou preparest before me in the presence of mine enemies;
Thou hast anointed my head with oil; my cup runneth over.
Surely goodness and mercy shall follow me all the
    days of my life;
And I shall dwell in the house of the Lord for ever.

THE TWELVE TRIBES OF ISRAEL

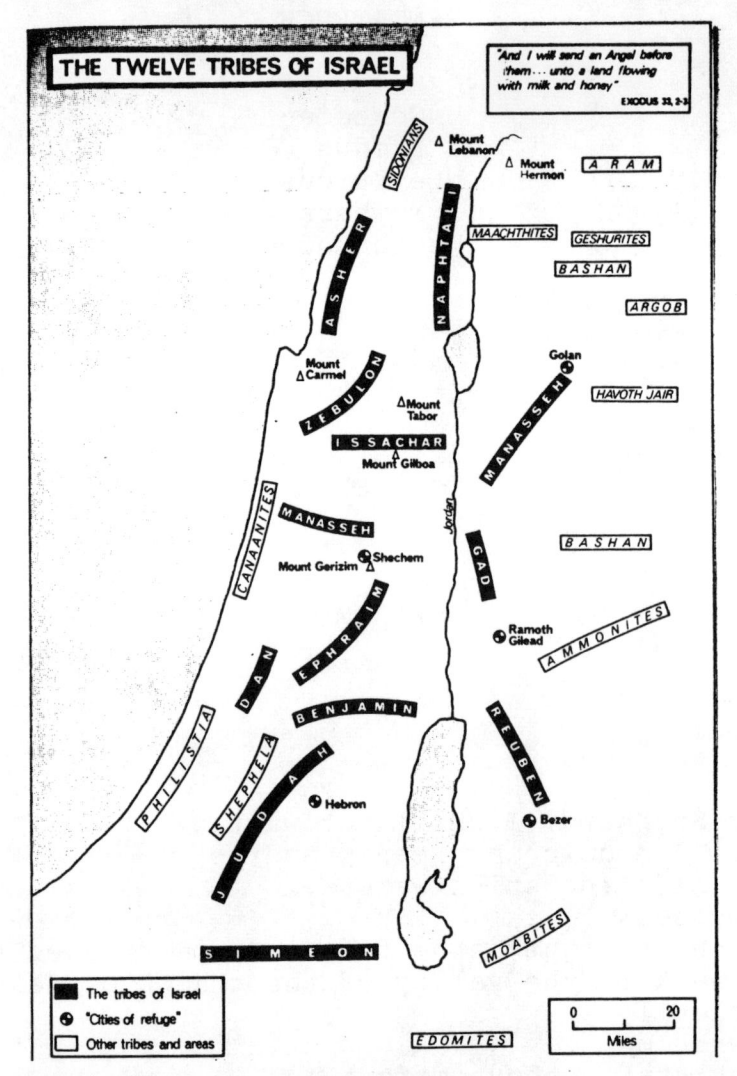

"And I will send an Angel before them... unto a land flowing with milk and honey"
EXODUS 33, 2-3

With permission from Martin Gilbert, *Jewish History Atlas*
MacMillan Printing, NY. 1969

    Judah
    Issachar
    Zebulon
    Reuben
    Simeon
    Gad
    Benjamin
    Dan
    Naphtali
    Asher
    Ephraim
    Manasseh

REFERENCES

Association of the Deaf in Israel. Israel.

Ausubel, N. The Book of Jewish Knowledge. New York: Crown Publishers, 1964.

Bridger, D. The New Jewish Encyclopedia. Behrman House, Inc. 1962.

Burstein, A. The Illustrated New Concise Jewish Encyclopedia. New York: KTAV Publishing, 1978.

Cherney, I. My Haggadah. New York: Behrman House, Inc., 1986.

Cokely, D. & Baker, C. American Sign Language: A Teacher's Resource Text on Grammar and Culture. Silver Spring, MD: TJ Publishers, 1980.

Gilbert, M. Jewish History Atlas. New York: MacMillan Publishing Co., Inc., 1969.

The Holy Scriptures. Philadelphia: Jewish Publication Society, 1944.

Isaacson, B. Dictionary of the Jewish Religion. New York: Bantam Books, 1979.

Kenner, M. (Ed.) The Jewish Deaf (12 vols.). New York: Society for the Welfare of the Jewish Deaf, 1915-1924, 1930-1932.

Kertzer, M. What Is A Jew? New York: Collier Books, 1978.

Markowitz, S. What You Should Know About Jewish Religion, History, Ethics, and Culture. New York: Citadel Press, 1955.

Namir, Sella, Rimor, & Schlesinger. Dictionary of Sign Language of the Deaf in Israel. Jerusalem, Israel: Ministry of Social Welfare, 1977.

Rosten, L. The Joys of Yiddish. New York: Pocket Books, 1973.

Samuel, E. Your Jewish Lexicon. New York: Union of American Hebrew Congregations, 1982.

Schein, J. & Waldman, L. The Deaf Jew in the Modern World. New York: KTAV Publishing House, Inc., 1986.

Shosteck, P. _A Lexicon of Jewish Cooking_. Chicago: Contemporary Books, 1979.

Siegel, Strassfeld, & Strassfeld. _The First Jewish Catalogue_. Philadelphia: Jewish Publication Society, 1973.

Sternberg, M. _American Sign Language: A Comprehensive Dictionary_. New York: Harper & Row, 1981.

Strassfeld, S. & Strassfeld, M. _The Second Jewish Catalogue_. Philadelphia: Jewish Publication Society, 1976.

White Mare, Inc. & Silver, A. _Let's...SIGN!_ Woodstock, NY: White Mare, Inc., 1985.

INDEX

Key to Abbreviations:
   I - Illustration   s. - singular   m. - masculine
   s.g. - sign gloss   pl. - plural   f. - feminine

A

"A great miracle happened there." 60
Aaron 2
Abraham I(2)-13; s.g.-15
"Ad me´ah ve´esrim!" 101
Adam and Eve I-2
   Adam and Havah 2
Adonai 112; 120
Adonai Ehad 120
Adonai Elohenu 120
Afikoman 49
Aggadah 69; 77
Aharon 2
Ahashverosh 62
Akdamut 52
Akedah 41
Al Het 42
Alijah 105; 138
All Vows 43
Amen 112
Amidah 112; I-113; 138
Anahnu Korim 112
Angel(s) 3
Anniversary of Death 103
Anti-Semites 88
Antiochus 59
Arab 105; I-106
Aramaic 92
Aravah 54
Arba´ah Minim 54
Arba Imahot 10
Arba Kanfot 36
Arba Kosot 49
Arba Kushiyot 47
Arey Ha-Halukah 25
Arey Ha-Kikkar 21
Ark of the Covenant 19; 113
   Aron Ha-Berit 19; 113
Aron Ha-Kodesh 142
Art Thou I-115
Aseret Yemai Teshuvah 41
Ashamnu 42
Ashkenazim 89

Attah 125
Avelut 102
Averah 69
Avodah 42; 147
Avodah Zarah 26
Avot 13
Avraham Avinu 13

B

Ba´al Teki´ah 40
Baal Shem Tov 71
Baal Teshuvah 69; 105
Babylonia 19
Bagel 148
Baitzah 46
Bar/Bat Mitzvah 96; I-97
Barekhu 113
Barukh Attah 114
Basar Kosher 79
Bath-Sheba 3
   Bat-Sheva 3
Bavel 19
Bavli 77
Bedikat 57
Beersheba I-20
   Be´er Sheva 20
Before Common Era (B.C.E.) 70
Benai Mitzvan 96
Benai Yisra´el 3; 8;15
Benediction 113
Berakhah 113
Berit 116
Berit Milah; Bris I-94
Besamim (Kufsat Besamim) 134
Bet Ha-Mikdash 26
Bet Ha-Tefutsot 111
Bet Hayyim or Bet Olam 101
Bet Knesset 146
Bet Lehem 20
Bet Midrash 146
Bet Tefilah 146

Beth El 20
Bethlehem 20; I(2)-21
Bialy 148
Bible 113; I(2)-114; 138
Bikkurim 52
Bimah 138; I-139
Binding of Isaac 41
Birkat Ha-Nerot 115
Birkat Ha-Mazon -115
Birkhot Ha-Torah 115
Blessed; Blessing(s) 113; 114; I-115
Blessing for Wine 128
Blintz 148
Bodek 81
Booth 53
Borscht 149
Breaking the Glass 99
Breastplate 139
Bride 98
Bringing in the Bride 100

C

Cain, Abel and Seth 3
Canaan 21
Candelabrum 110; 136
Candles: See Kindling the Candles; Lighting of the Candles
Cantor 139; I-140
Canopy I(2)-99
Caro, Joseph 76
Carp 149
Cemetery 101
Chicken 149
Chickpeas 149
Children of Israel 3; 115
Choir I-140
Chopped Liver 149
Chrain 151
Chutzpah 156
Circumcision I-94
Cities of the Plain 21
Closing 43
Codes of Jewish Law -76
Collective Farm 109
Commandments 121
Common Era 70

Confirmation 97; I-98
Congregation 141
Consecrate s.g.-116
Conservative I(2)-73
Conversion 78
Covenant I-116
Crown 142
Cup of Benediction 33
Custom 78

D

Dairy 79
Dati 70; 71
Daven 144
David I-4
  David Ha-Melekh 4
Day of Atonement 41
Day of Holocaust 65
Dayenu 50
Dead Sea 22
Deborah 4
Dedicating a New Home 33
Devorah 4
Diaspora 106; I-107; 111
Dietary Laws 79
Divine Commandment 86
Divorce; Divorce Certificate 101
Dowry 100
Dreidel I-60

E

Egg 149
Egg Cream 150
Egypt I-22
Eighteen Benedictions 112; Appendix
Eighth Day of Assembly 57
Eilat I-107
Elijah I-5
Elijah's Chair 95
Elijah's Cup 50
Eliyahu 5
Elohim 117
Engagement 98
Erev 39

Eretz Ha-Kodesh 26
Eretz Yisra´el 27, 29
Erusin 98
Esau 5
   Esav 5
Eser Makkot 50
Ester Ha-Malkah 61
Esther I-62
Eternal Light I-141
Eternity 116
Etrog 54
Exile 24
Exodus I(2)-23
Ezra 5

F

Falafel 108
Farfel 150
Fast 43; 67
Father 116
Fathers 13
Feast of Lots 61
Feast of Weeks 52
Feh! 156
Festival of Booths 53
Festival of Dedication 58
Festival of Unleavened Bread 44
Finials 145
Fir Kashes 47
Five Books of Moses 117
Fleishig 80
Flekn 150
Food Fit for Jewish Eating 79
Forbidden Food 81
Four Cups of Wine 49
Four Mothers 10
Four Questions 47
Four Species 54
Fringes 37
Fruit of the Vine 117
Frum I-71

G

Galilee 24
   Galil 24
Galut 24; 106
Gan Ayden 24
Garden of Eden 24
Gefilte Fish 150
Gehakte Leber 149
Gelilah 141
Gelt 60
Gemarah 77
Gematria 82
Gentile 141
Get 101
Glatt 79
God I-117
Going Up 105
Golah 24
Goliath 6
   Golyat 6
Gomorrah 20
Goulash 150
Goy 156
Greps 156
Grieven 150
Grogger I-63
Groom 99
Gut Shabbes 156
Gut Yontoff 67; 156

H

Ha-Motzi 115; 128; 134
Had Gadya 51
Hadass 54
Hadlakut Ha-Nerot 136
Haftarah 97; 118
Hag Ha-Aviv 44
Hag Sameah 67
Hagbah 142
Haggadah 47
   Haggadot (pl.) 47
   Haggadah Shel Pesah 47
Haifa I-108
Hakhnassat Kallah 100
Hakkafot 55
Halakhah 76
Hallah 134; 150
Hallel 121

Halleluyah I-118
Halutz (s.); Halutzim (pl.) 108
Halvah 151
Haman 63
Haman's Pockets 63
Hamantaschen 63; I-64
Hametz 51
Hanukat Ha-Bayit 32; 82
Hanukkah I-58
Hanukkiyah 58
Happy Holiday 67
Har Sinai 30
Har Tzeyon 32
Haroset 46
Hasidim 71
  Hasidut 71
Hatan 99
Hatan Berayshit 56
Hatan Torah 56
Hatikvah 109; 131
Havdallah 134; I(2)-135
Hayt 124
Hayyim 83; 119
Hazeret 46
Hazzan 139
Hear O Israel 118
Heaven 118
Hebrew I-8; 92
  Hebrew(s) 6
Hebron I-25
Hekhsher 81
Heritage I-82
Herring 151
Herzl, Theodore 91
Hevron 25
Hidden Matzah 49
High Holy Days 39
High Priest I-6
Hol Ha-Mo'ed 67
Holiday 68
Holocaust I-63
  Day of Holocaust 63
Holy; Holiness I-119
Holy Ark 142
Holy Cities of the Halukah 25
Holy of Holies 26
Holy Land 26
Holy Scriptures (See Bible)
  I-114; 142

Holy Temple s.g.-26
Holy Tongue 92
Holoptosches 155
Honey 151
Horah s.g.-109
Horseradish 151
Hoshanah Rabbah 55
Hoshanot 55
House of God 20
Hov; Hovah 75
Humash 147
Huppah I(2)-99

I

Idol/Idolatry 26
Isaac I-14; s.g.-15
Ishmael 7
Israel I(2)-7; 14; 27; 109; 119
  Israel, See also Jew(ish)
  Hebrew, Israel I-8
Israeli(s) -109
  Israelites I-7
Israel Independence Day 66
"It would have been
  sufficient." 50
Ivri(m) 6
Ivrit 92

J

Jacob 14; s.g.-15
Jericho 27
Jerusalem I-28; 109
Jew(ish) I(2)-8
  Jew(s); Jewish 8; 83
  Jewry; Judaism s.g.-83
Jewish Arbor Day 61
Jewish Law 76
Jewish New Year 39; s.g.-40
Jordan 28
Joseph 9
Joy of the Sabbath 135; 136
Judah/Judea 29
Judah the Maccabee 59

K

Kabbalah 77
Kabbalat Shabbat 135
Kaddish 3; s.g.-101
Kadesh 116
Kallah 98
Kallat Bereyshit 56
Kallat Torah 56
Kaplan, Mordecai 74
Kapotah I-72
Karpas I-46
Kasha 151
Kasher 79
Kashrut 79
Kayim, Hevel and Shet 3
Kedushah 119
Keesay Eliyahu 95
Kena´an 21
Ke´arah 46
Keri´ah -102
Keter 142
Ketubah 100
Kibbutz (s.) 109;
   Kibbutzim (pl.) 109
Kiddush 83; 136
Kiddush Cup 33
Kiddushin 98
Kindle 136
Kindling the Candles 129
King 119
King Ahasuerus 62
Kippah (See Yarmulka)
   I-33; 37; 147
Kishke 151
Klupper 156
Klutz 156
Knaidlach 152
Knesset s.g.-110
Knish 152
Kodesh Ha-Kodashim 26
Kohanim See Kohen 9; 16; 142
Kohen I-9; 16; 142; I-143
Kohen Gadol 6
Kol Ha-Ne´rim 57
Kol Nidre 43
Kos Shel B´rakhah 33
Kos Shel Elijahu 50
Kosher 79; I(2)-80; 156
Kosher Le-Pesah 79
Kotel Ma´aravi Western Wall 32
Kugel 152
Kvetch 156

L

Ladino 92
Lag B´Omer I-66
Land of Israel 29
Latkes 59
L´Chayim 84
Le-Kadesh 123
Leah 10
   Le´ah 10
Leshanah Ha-Ba´ah
   Be-Yerushalayim 51
Leshanah Ha-Ba´ah
   Be-Yerushalayim Ha-Benuyah 51
Le-Shanah Tovah Tikatevu 40
Leaven 51
Leshon Ha-Kodesh 92
Levi 9
   Levi´im 9
   Levites 9
Levivah (s.); Levivot (pl.) 59
Life 83; I-84; 119
   "Life to 120 years." 101
Lighting of the Candles 136
Lokshen 153
Lord I-120
Lot 10
Lox 152
Lulav (See Sukkot) I-53; 54

M

Ma´ariv 14; 145
Macher 156
Magen David 35
"Mah nish-tannah ha-lailah
   ha-zeh?" 47
Mahzor 34; 68
Maimonides, Moses 76

Malakh(im) 3
Mantle 143
Mappah 143
Maror I-46; I-49
Marriage 98
Masada I-29
Mashgiah 81
Mashiah 11; 120

Matanot Le´Evyonim 65
Matriarchs 10
Matzah (also see Passover 1)
  45; I-48
  Matzot (pl.) 48
Matzo Balls 152
Maven 156
"May you be inscribed for a new
  year!" 40
Mazel 156
Mazel Tov 101
Meat 80
Medinat Yisrael 110
Meditate 120
Megillah I-64
Mehitzah 143
Mehren Tzimmes 155
Melekh 116; 119;
  Melakhim (pl.) 119
Menorah (See Hanukkah) I-58;
  110; 136; 143
Mensh or Mentch 156
Menuhah 136
Meshugga 156
Messiah I-11; 120
Metzadah 29
Metzia 156
Mezzuzah I-34
Midrash 84
Mikveh I-84; I-85; 101
Milchik 79
Minhag 78
Minhah 14; 145
Minyan I-85; 144
Miriam 11
  Miryan 11
Mishebayrakh 120
Mishkan or Ohel Mo´ed 32
Mishloah Manot 65
Mishnah 77
Mishneh Torah 76
Mit Varnitchkes 151
Mitzrayim 22

Mitzvah 86
  Mitzvot (pl.) 121
Mohel 95
Money 60
Mordecai 62
  Mordehai 62
Moses I-12
  Moshe 12
Mount Sinai I-30
Mount Zion I-30; 32
Mourning 102
Moving to Israel 110
Musaf 145
"My Dreidel" 131

N

Naches 156
Naming 95
Naomi 12
Nedunyah; Naden 100
Ne´ilah 43
Ner Tamid 144
"Nes gadol hayah sham." 60
Neshamah 124
Nevi´im 16
Next Year in Jerusalem 51
Ninth Day of Av 67
Nissu´in 100
Noodge 157
Noodles 152
Nosh 157
Nu? 157
Nudnik 157

O

Ohel Mo´ed 32
Oil 59
Olam 126
Old Testament 144
Omer 66
"One Kid" 51
Oneg Shabbat 136
Oral Law 76; 77
Order 44
Orthodox (See also Frum)
  I(2)-70
Oy, oy vey 157

P

Palestine 30
Paras 30
Par´oh 15
Parokhet 144
Parve 80
Passover 44; I(3)-45
Patriarchs 13
Payah; Payot (pl.) 72
Payess I-72
Penitent 69
Pentateuch 121; 144
"People of the Torah" s.g.-8

Peree Ha-Gafen 117
Persia 38
Perushim 15
Pesah 44
Pharaoh I-15
Pharisees 15
Phylacteries I-34; 36
Pidyon Ha-Ben 96
Pike 153
Pilgrim Festivals 44
Pioneer(s) 108
Pious 71
Pomegranate 153
Praise 121
Pray 121; I(2)-122
   Prayer; Worship; Services 144
Prayer Book 35
Prayer Shawl (See Tallit)
   I-35; 36
Priest(s) 9; (See High Priest
   for root sign) 6; 16
Processionals 55
Prophets 16
"Psalm 23" Appendix
Pulpit 138
Pumpernickel 153
Purim 61
Pushke 35; 137

Q

Queen Esther 61; I-62

R

Ra´ashan 63
Rabbi I-145
Rachel 10
   Rahel 10
Ram´s Horn 40
Rebecca 10
Reconstructionism I-74
Red Sea 31
Redemption of the First Born 96
Reform 74; I(2)-75
Rejoicing of the Torah 55
Religious; Religion I-86
   (See also Frum)
Repent I-42; 121; I-122
   (See also Yom Kippur)
Rimmonim 145
Ritual 86; I-87; 123
Ritual Bath 101

Rivkah 10
Rochel 10
Rock 123
"Rock of Ages" 132
Root 16
Rosh Hashanah 39; s.g.-40
Rosh Hodesh I-68
Ruth 16
Rye 154

S

Sabbath I(2)-133
Sabra 110
Sacrifice I-123
Sadducees 17
Salt Water 46
Samson 17
Samuel 17
Sanctify 123
Sandek 95
Sarah 10
Saul 17
Scattering 106
Schav 154
Schechter, Solomon 73

Schmaltz 154
Scroll 64
Sea of Reeds 31
Sea of the Plain 22
Search for Leaven 51
Seder 44
Seder Plate 46
Sedom Va-Amorah 31
Sefirat Ha-Omer 66
Selihot 41
Seltzer 154
Seminary I-87
Semites 8
Sephardim 89
Servant 146
Services (See Pray for sign) I-122; 145
Se´udat Mitzvah 95
Seven Blessings 100
Seven-day Mourning 102
Seventh Day of Sukkot 55
Sevivon 60
Shabbos 133
   Shabbot 133
Shaharit 13; 145
Shaloch Mones 65
Shalom 123; 132
Shalom Aleichem 123; 157
Shalom Zahar 94
Shalosh Regalim 44
Shamayim 118
Shammash 58; 146
Shanah Tovah 40
Shaul 17
Shavuot I-52
Shaygetz 157
Shehecheyanu 130
Shehitah 81
Sheitl 73
Shel Rosh 36
Shelomo Ha-Melekh 17
Sheloshim 102
Shema 130
Shema Yisrael 118
Shemen 59
Shemini Atzeret 57
Shemoneh Esreh 112
Shemuel 17
Sheva Broches 100;
   Sheva Berakhot 100

Shevatim 18
Shikker 157
Shiksa 157
Shimson; Shimson Ha-Gibbor 17
Shivah 102; I-103
Shlemazel 157
Shlemeil 157
Shlepp 157
Shloomp 157
Shmooze 157
Shmutz 157
Shofar I-40
Shohet 81
   Shohet u´vodek 81
Shomer Shabbat 137
Shroud 103
Shtreimel I-72
Shul 146
Shulkhan Arukh 76
Shushan Purim 65
Siddur 35
Simhah 88
Simhat Bat 96
Simhat Torah 55; I-56
Sin 69; I-124
Skullcap 33
Small Tallit 36
Smoked Fish 154
Sodom and Gomorrah 31
Solomon 17; I-18
Soul I-124
Sour Cream 154
Spice Box 134; 137
Sponge Cake 155
Standing Silent Prayer 112
Star of David 35; I-36
State of Israel 110
Story of Passover 47
Strudel 155
Stuffed Cabbage 155
Stuffed Derma 151
Sufganiyot 59
Sukkah 53
Sukkot I-53
Suria 31
Synagogue I-146
Syria I(2)-31

174

T

Tabernacle 32
Tahrihin 103
Talmud 77; 147
Tallit 36; I-38
   Tallit Katan 36
Tanakh 138
Tashlih 39
Teacher 145
Tefilah 144
Tefillin 36; I-38
Tefillin Shel Yad 36
Tefutsot 111
Tel Aviv I-111
Temple I-146
Ten Commandments I-125; Appendix
Ten Days of Penitence 41
Ten Plagues 50
Tena´im 98
Terefah 81
Tevilah 84
Thee, Thou, Thine I-125
Tisha B´Av 67
Torah I-126; 129-130; 147
Tradition 77; I(2)-88
Traif 81
Tu B´Shevat 61
Twelve Tribes 18; Appendix
Tzadik 90
Tzedakah 89; I-90
Tzedakah Box 35; 137
Tzedukim 17
Tzeyon 127
Tzimmes 155
Tzitz 139
Tzitzit 37
Tzom 43; 67

U

Universe I-126
Unleavened Bread 48
Unveiling 103

V

Vashti 62

W

Wedding Contract 100
Western Wall (Wailing Wall) s.g.-32
Whitefish 155
"Why is this night different from all other nights?" 47
Wise, Rabbi Isaac Meyer 74
Worship 147
Wrapper 143
Written Law 76

Y

Ya´akov 14
Yad 147
Yahadut 83
Yahrzeit s.g.-103
Yam Ha-Melah 22
Yam Soof 31
Yamin Nora´im 39
Yarden 28
Yarmulka 37; I-38; 147
Yehuda Ha-Makabee 57
Yehudah 29
Yehudi(m) (pl.) 8; 83;
   Yehudi (m.) 83;
   Yehudiah (f.) 83
Yente 157
Yeriho 27
Yerushalayim 28; 109
Yerushalmi 77
Yeshiva 90; I-91
Yetzait Mitzrayim 23
Yiddish 93
Yiddishkeit 83
Yishma´el 7
Yisra´el (Yisrael) 7; 14; 27; 119
   Yisra´eli (m.) 109
   Yisra´elit (f.) 109
   Yisraelim (pl.) 109
Yitzhak 14
Yizkor s.g.-104

Yom Ha-Atzmaut 66
Yom Ha-Din (Day of Judgement) 38
Yom Ha-Shoah 65
Yom Teru´ah (Day of Blowing the Shofar) 38
Yom Ha-Zikaron (Day of Remembrance) 38
Yom Kippur 41; I-42
Yom Tov 68
Yosef 9

Z

Zafti 157
Zeman Herutenu 44
Zero´ah 46
Zhlob 157
Zion 127
Zionism 91
Zoftig 157
Zohar 77